MW01103546

THE
dependent

A MEMOIR OF MARRIAGE & THE MILITARY

The Dependent
A Memoir of Marriage and the Military

Danielle Daniel

LATITUDE 46
PUBLISHING

Copyright © 2016 by Danielle Daniel

All rights reserved. No part of this book may be used or reproduced in any manner whatsoever without the prior written permission of the publisher, except in the case of brief quotation embodied in reviews.

Library and Archives Canada Cataloguing in Publication

Daniel, Danielle, 1974-, author
The dependent : a memoir of marriage and the military
/ Danielle Daniel.

ISBN 978-0-9949183-4-5 (paperback)

1. Daniel, Danielle, 1974- --Marriage. 2. Daniel, Steve.
3. Army spouses--Canada--Biography. 4. Military dependents--
Canada--Biography. 5. Canada--Armed Forces--Parachute troops--
Biography. 6. Women and the military. 7. Canada. Canadian Armed
Forces--Military life. I. Title.

This is a work of creative nonfiction. The events are portrayed to the best of Danielle Daniel's memory. While all the stories in this book are true, some names and identifying details have been changed to protect the privacy of the people involved.

U773.D36 2016   355.0092   C2016-903196-9

Printed and bound in Canada on 100% recycled paper.

BOOK DESIGN:
Cover Design: Fuel Multimedia and Gerry Kingsley
Author photo: Gerry Kingsley

PUBLISHED BY:

LATITUDE 46
PUBLISHING

Latitude 46 Publishing
info@latitude46publishing.com
Latitude46publishing.com

For Steve
To who we were and who we are.
And to who we are always becoming.

"Nobody has ever measured, not even poets,
how much the heart can hold."

— Zelda Fitzgerald

"I am no bird; and no net ensnares me:
I am a free human being with an independent will."
— Charlotte Brontë, Jane Eyre

contents

1 | Voluntold

I never told him about the recurring blow I felt to my stomach, the one that often stopped me from taking another step as I walked towards my school to teach for the day, even when he was finally back from Afghanistan, safe and sound. I couldn't shake the sense that he was still in danger. Or the recurring dreams in which I'd hear his voice calling out to me in distress, while he snored by my side. I would reach for his body, poking him with my finger, then try to will myself back asleep while doom floated over me, an invisible gas. This continued for months, and I never said anything to anyone.

"Come and dance with me," he said, pulling my sleeve.

"Not now," I shook my arm loose from his grip. "These report cards won't get done on their own, you know."

"Just leave it for five minutes," he said, dragging me away from the chair. He pushed his hips against mine. "Don't you still like my moves?"

I gave in to his whim. I humoured him. I tucked my arms under his and wrapped them around his back, feeling his muscles moving under my hands. I slumped my head on his shoulder and watched the afternoon sun pouring through our patio doors.

That was the weekend before he left on course—another course he was *voluntold* to complete, for his other family. The course he'd been working towards his whole life, like all the others. Steve was so eager to become a qualified free-fall jumpmaster. I couldn't believe he was going away again. We had already spent nine months apart that year.

"I'll be home on weekends, it won't be so bad," he whispered in my ear as our legs criss-crossed along the living room floor.

1

Why wasn't I given more? Why couldn't I dream of the part where he falls from the sky? The part where he crashes to the ground? Where he breaks his back and is instantly paralyzed from the waist down—and never walks again?

Our lives severed: Before and After.

When we moved into our second house, I bought a sleigh bed for us. Steve didn't want me to buy it, said we couldn't afford it. I bought it anyway because I just had to have it. I knew I would never find another one as beautiful—solid wood with a dark stain.

"Danielle, what were you thinking?" he said, his voice taut with anger as the delivery men set it up in our bedroom. "We already have enough expenses."

"I make my own money, Steve, and that bed was a steal. It'll cost double when it's finally the right time."

"Well, at least we'd be able to afford it then. It's called being responsible."

"You're not the one doing the shopping. You don't know how much a bed costs, and this bed was a bargain. Trust me."

That night, after we unpacked, we fell into our new bed.

"Oh God, I'm exhausted," I said. "I can't believe how much we did in one day."

"You hauled ass, private, and you know, this bed doesn't suck. It's actually comfortable."

"Really? So you aren't mad at me anymore?"

"Well, I wouldn't go that far, but I guess after six years of marriage we deserve a real bed. But we should test it out to be sure." He kissed my neck.

"I don't know. I think you still need to apologize for freaking out about it," I teased.

"Why don't I just show you I'm sorry," he said as he rolled on top of me, muffling my squeals of laughter.

I counted. I slept in that bed two years and one month. He slept in it three months plus a week. I'm glad I didn't wait for the right time to buy that bed.

I remember the day the young kid (he was more like twenty), with his pants hanging low and his loud T-shirt, came to our house, the one we had built, to dismantle our sleigh bed and replace it with one like those you see on TV. The Tempur-Pedic kind that old people rave about on those late night infomercials.

"You'll sleep so much better," Steve said. "You won't feel me move around at night."

"You're probably right," I said.

"And my body won't hurt so much sleeping on this mattress. You'll have your own remote control. Plus, reading will be easier. We won't need a thousand pillows on the bed anymore."

I like a thousand pillows.

Steve wasn't home that day, so he didn't hear me yell at the kid when I walked into our bedroom and saw that he'd set up the new Tempur-Pedic beds detached from each other. Two singles, side by side with five feet apart to walk through the middle. It was like being in Nanny and Pépère's room. His side and her side—single and separate. Their marriage, loveless and habitual.

"I'm not an eighty-seven-year-old grandma, buddy!" I shouted. "Put those beds together now!"

The kid looked stunned, wiped his forehead, and got on it right away. I ran downstairs and wept in the bathroom while the boy connected the two beds with a metal bar and several bolts. Steve still wasn't home; he'd had group work for one of his business classes at the college. I tried not to cry when he returned that night to our new beds with his-and-her remote controls. I tried not to show him how crushed I was that our wooden sleigh bed was now in pieces in the basement.

Our new beds were a lot like the ones we'd slept on in Europe during his three-week leave from Bosnia. The time I flew to Paris to meet him and we backpacked for three weeks across France, Italy, and Spain. Two single beds in one room. We laughed when we saw them and wondered why Europeans had so many hotels with single beds. We pushed them together, but no matter how much we tried to keep them from splitting apart, one of us always managed to feel the gap under our back. We were never able to get close, like two people spread apart by a lie. The line was always there.

Three years later, I still detested our separate beds, maybe even more than when they had arrived. I hated that I had to buy single sheets for his side and my side. I hated that, most nights, only our hands touched as we met halfway at the gap that divided us. I hated that a metal rod linked these separate beds and that only guests used our beautiful sleigh bed. Sometimes I lay on it, but never for long.

Steve tells me that when he dreams, he is usually walking. When I dream, he is never walking; he is sitting in his wheelchair, the one that is always with us. I wish I could at least be standing hand in hand with him in my dreams, but that never happens. Instead, we are both in wheelchairs, struggling to get somewhere: we circle around the pool at our local community centre on opposite sides, our hands driving the wheels forward while, in the pool, children and parents point and stare. We continue, around and around, unable to find a way to get into the water. And nobody offers to help.

I despised his wheelchair in the beginning, a permanent symbol of everything we had lost. This metal chair took up so much space and seemed cruel as it crushed my toes if I didn't pay attention. How awkward it was for me to lift it and make it fit in the back of my car while people gawked. Now this unwanted chair has become as common as hanging up my jacket in the closet.

I remember the way he walked, slightly pigeon-toed. How he always liked to wear big boots, even on leave. How he polished them every morning before leaving for work. Now his shoes always stay looking like new, the soles clean and dry, unscuffed.

If only I had left the report cards for one more day. We could have danced until the sun went down and played all of our favourite songs.

2 | Phase One

Phase One: Stage 1: Anticipation of Loss

PRE-DEPLOYMENT
(Time Frame: 1–6 weeks prior to departure)

Common Reactions

- Fluctuations in energy levels and mood
- Fantasizing
- Feelings of sadness, anger, excitement, restlessness
- Anxiety, tension, frustration, resentment, depression

CF Deployment Handbook: A Practical Guide for Families

It was happening again. I felt it building all week. Short breaths and long sighs as he walked through the house getting ready for work. In the basement, too, for hours at a time, where he'd been checking lists and packing kit: green things in green bags. There was no access to him. Like looking at the ferry slipping away into the distance. You could jump into the water, but there would be no point. It won't turn around, so you shake your fist and walk away. Finally, I couldn't ignore it. Steve and I were watching TV together, something we seldom did. Sitting was a waste of time, he said, no matter what you're doing.

"What are you looking for?" He was flipping through the channels, back and forth, at warp speed.

"Anything but this crap," he said.

"Pick a channel already. Your flicking's gonna give me a seizure."

He pitched the remote into my lap, and walked out to the garage.

"Where you going?" I yelled as he slammed the door.

I grabbed a cushion and flung it across the room, making Molly, our German shepherd, jump to her feet. I snatched the remote from my lap, chucked it into the far corner of the couch and headed straight for the garage.

Like everything under his domain, the garage was tidy and organized. He made Martha Stewart look like an amateur. Perfect rows of bins all aligned and clearly marked in meticulous lettering with a black Sharpie. He ignored me as he reached for his motorcycle helmet. I plopped myself down on the riding lawn mower.

"What the hell is your problem today?" I asked.

"My problem? You're the bitchy one. We can't even watch TV without getting into it," he answered, spraying Windex on the visor.

"Get into it? I just asked you to commit to a channel. I wouldn't call that bitchy."

"No, you're never bitchy. My mistake."

"Well, maybe I'm just trying to get you plugged in for once."

"I am not going there today."

"You're so spaced out all the time—in another time zone already! It would be nice if we had an actual conversation once in a while. When will it be convenient for you, Master Corporal—sir?" He looked at me, not a single speck of love in his eyes. "It's no wonder women put their Tide boxes in the windows when their husbands are gone. At least then, somebody will pay attention to them!"

I knew I had gone too far. It wasn't at all what I wanted to say, but it was too late. My words were airborne.

His brown eyes glared at me, seeming ominously black. Without a word, he grabbed his keys, jumped into his truck, and drove away, spraying gravel as he spun the tires.

Now there I was, sitting on the floor, staring at the door and wishing I could hear the sound of the stupid truck crunching back into the driveway.

The cycle was in full swing. We had taken up our roles, the ones defined in our issued handbook: "Pre-Deployment is often harder than the actual separation. Spouses should expect higher levels of stress and conflict. This is common and should be understood as standard marital conduct prior to departure."

General Coping Suggestions

- Allow yourself to feel and express all emotional responses
- Encourage all family members to share their feelings
- Complete the Pre-Deployment checklist with your spouse
- Create opportunities for warm and lasting memories; take pictures
- Set realistic goals for yourself for the deployment period

CF Deployment Handbook: A Practical Guide for Families

Phase One. We both knew it would only worsen.

As an infantry soldier, Steve could be deployed at any time—and he lived for it. It's what he trained for every day. When you train for the Olympics, you want to go to the Olympics, at least once. The same goes for the army. You want to put your skills to the test. Playing GI Joe on the base field was not enough.

I had married into the army four years before. For better or for worse. There is no special clause in the marriage vows for military wives.

He came home a few hours later, after a workout at the gym on the base. That's what he did with his free time. At least he wasn't a drinker, I told myself. He took a shower and slept on the couch, without even entering the bedroom to get a change of clothes. I stayed awake, flipping from one side to other, and eventually tossed the comforter off the bed. Finally, I counted myself to sleep: how many nights we still had together before he left, how many more nights we would spend apart.

I started to isolate myself from friends in the last few weeks before he left. I didn't have the energy to reassure them, to convince them that I'd be fine this time.

Phase One: Stage 2: Detachment and Withdrawal

PRE-DEPLOYMENT
(Time Frame: 1 week prior to departure)

Common Reactions

- Reduced emotional and sexual intimacy
- Feelings of despair, hopelessness, impatience, numbness

General Coping Strategies

- Accept your feelings as normal reactions to challenging circumstances
- Communicate as openly and honestly as possible
- Be patient with yourself and family members
- Keep the last day free for family time
- Ignore rumours and rely on official sources of information

CF Deployment Handbook: A Practical Guide for Families

I wasn't like this all the time. Sure, some days I'd wake up mad at the world. As I marched through the grocery store, I'd curse at the music that filled the aisles, pathetic elevator tunes mixed with cheesy love songs. Everything aggravated me. I avoided pleasantries and despised the clerks who asked: "How are you today?" I didn't have the energy to say, "Fine." I usually forced a smile through my clenched teeth.

Other days, I felt like Wonder Woman. I flexed my muscles and conquered everything on my to-do list. I called Bell to change the long-distance plan, organized the closets, painted the trim in the office, called the oil guy to fill up the tank. I'd do it all.

Then, before I knew it, my Wonder Woman superpowers were gone. I couldn't bear to take out the garbage or fix the leak in the kitchen faucet. Pay the bills? Clean out the rotting food from the fridge? No way. I yelled at Steve for his lack of support around the house.

"Why am I the only one to handle all of the errands and responsibilities around here?" I ranted. "I work, too. I'm tired of dealing with everything on my own. Just me, myself, and I." And you haven't even left yet.

After the storm, the calm.

One week after our fight in the garage, I was ready to clear the air again. We hadn't discussed the argument. We hadn't had make-up sex.

The tension cut through the morning, slicing into my breathing space. I shut the cupboard doors harder than I needed to.

"Geez, take it easy over there," he said, stirring his oatmeal.

"I have a ton of things to do today and I'm not on leave, like you."

"What is that supposed to mean?" he said.

"It means I don't get time off from my employer to sort out my admin."

"Don't start this again."

"Start what?" I asked, triumphant that I'd roused a reaction at last.

"I knew this was coming," he said, widening his eyes and deepening his voice.

"Well, what do you expect? You haven't talked to me all week."

"You know, Dan, I've been thinking. Maybe you just don't have what it takes to be an army wife anymore."

"Well, Steve, maybe I've just reached my limit. Aren't you the one who says everyone has a magic number? Three tours. Four years of marriage. Eight years together. Take your pick."

"Well, maybe you should pack up and leave then!"

He'd seen it at least a hundred times before. Sometimes a buddy got the letter overseas, and sometimes he just came home to an empty house. This didn't happen only in the movies. This happened for real and I knew it terrified him.

"Why do you always end up saying that? Is that what you really want?" I asked, the tears coming again, my wall breached too.

"Maybe it is."

They said this was normal. It was in our handbook, *Military Families, Strength Behind the Uniform*, prefaced by soothing words: "You may find hope and reassurance in this model and the suggested coping strategies, with the knowledge that many others share your responses to this challenging experience." But this was our third tour and I was still waiting for it to get easier. Croatia: check. Bosnia: check. Now Bosnia again. I didn't find hope or reassurance in collective suffering.

I slammed the front door, jumped into my minivan, and drove around, unable to reach a destination. I drove through the damp streets, grateful it was raining. I couldn't go anywhere or see anyone. I was afraid others would think I wasn't coping. I was petrified that my marriage would be one of the statistics after that tour. Eighty percent of military marriages end in divorce. That's what the clerks told Steve's unit during one of their pre-deployment debriefs. Even on a good day, the odds were against us. Finally, I pulled into a car dealership parking lot and sobbed. I let it all out, surprised at how much pain was underneath the fury. After that long, I should have had a thicker skin. I should have been able to tolerate that way of life. I had done it before. I knew what to expect. But maybe that was the problem. I didn't want my husband to leave for six months for a country that was hurting its own people, where he could be killed while I waited and prayed that it wouldn't happen. I didn't feel like holding my breath for the next six months.

"Maybe he's right. Maybe I don't have what it takes anymore." I said this out loud, testing the words in the silence of the van. Who could I talk to? Most of the people I knew were going through the same relentless progression of emotions; sympathy was hard to find. Too often, the women in my circle licked their own wounds and compared their severity rather than supporting one another. This was a myth—the support network did not exist. Not even among the ones who knew exactly how it felt.

I didn't know what else to do with myself. Utterly desperate, I started to pray. "Hello up there—you know I'm not religious. And I'm far from being a good Catholic. But I do believe. So I'm asking if you can help me here. How am I going to manage this time? A sign would be good. I'd take that."

I found a used tissue in my purse and blew my nose on a clean corner. I looked at myself in the mirror. God, I looked like hell. I raked my fingers through my hair.

During the last deployment, while I stood in line at the post office, a little girl saw me like this. I was sending a care package off to Croatia, where Steve was deployed for almost seven months. It had been a difficult tour. We were newly married; he left two weeks after our wedding day. I stood in line, holding the parcel, carefully and lovingly packaged, with some of his favourite candy bars, books, photos, and other surprises. This was before the days of email, digital cameras, and iPhones. I would send him cards and letters on pretty stationary that took me hours to pick out. Letters could take two months to arrive and, of course, the news was always old. Steve would write to me in cursive on blue United Nations envelopes and number each one. Sometimes 22 would arrive before 20 and I'd tear into it, unable to wait to read the letters in consecutive order. He would draw doodles in the margins—hearts with S + D and mini-portraits of himself with big muscles and captions like, "Tell all boys to stay away from you."

So there I stood, holding the package that had taken me a week to prepare. It was an off day, a hard one. No specific reason, just one of those days when I felt the heaviness in my heart. A little girl with blond, curly hair, about eight years old, was staring at me as she stood beside her mother. She wore a dance leotard under her winter jacket, with white winter boots that had white pompom tassels on the ties. I didn't recognize her; she wasn't a student from the school where I taught. Usually, I smiled at kids and made eye contact. But that time, I couldn't. I was so tired and felt such pressure bearing down on my chest. I didn't have it in me to feign even a smile.

The girl pulled on her mother's sleeve and whispered loud enough for everyone to hear: "Mom, she's so sad."

I squeezed the care package against my chest and fixed my gaze on the floor. Everyone turned at once to look at me as I counted the tiles surrounding my feet.

"That's enough, Hailey," the mother said. She glanced at me, raising her eyebrows with apology. I flashed a brief, awkward smile, checked the time on my watch, and felt my legs buckle. Sometimes the sadness was so ripe, I swooned with its heavy secret. Even if I tried to hide it, children could always sense it. I knew this as a teacher. They could smell truth like dogs. Usually, I stayed home. Weekdays were easier, since I was busy with my students. But weekends were for families, and my closest family was a four-hour drive away. Instead, I would stay in bed, hidden under the blankets with a book—quarantined. My sorrow felt like a disease nobody wanted to catch, not in that military town.

No divine signs had come my way. I drove home slowly from the dealership, manoeuvring through the deserted streets like a drunk driver trying to look sober. The sky was lightening just a little in the east as I pulled into the driveway of our white bungalow. Our house was small, a fixer-upper. We had put the down payment on it the year before using the money from my final paycheque before summer vacation and our collected RRSP contributions. We lived meagrely off of Steve's military pay all summer, barely making it to September. But it was worth it. That little white house and the field that surrounded us was our small piece of heaven, remote from everything military. I opened the door, putting the keys on the counter. The house felt empty; the stillness, palpable. The lights were all off and the refrigerator hummed the way it always did at night. Steve's wallet was on the table—he was home. I walked towards the bedroom, anxious to clean my face, wondering what his mood would be. Would the arguing continue or was he just as worn out as I was? I'd been gone most of the night. It was after ten.

He was speaking to someone on the phone. I knew it wasn't good—I felt it in my stomach.

When he hung up, he said, "Everyone has been moved up by two weeks. We're leaving Friday."

"This Friday, like five days from today?"

"This Friday," he answered in his non-negotiable tone. My heart shattered. Tiny sharp pieces splattering my insides, leaving tiny holes. I searched his eyes but no tears surfaced and no further words came. I turned and ambled to the bathroom. Looking in the mirror, I scrubbed my face in harsh circles. I brushed my teeth slowly, avoiding the moment when I'd have to go to bed.

Phase Two: Emotional Disorganization

DURING DEPLOYMENT
(Time Frame: First 6 weeks of deployment)

Common Reactions

- Magical thinking – believing the impossible or unlikely
- Sleep and appetite disturbances
- Feelings of relief, guilt, anger, numbness, depression
- Confusion, disorganization, indecision, loneliness
- Vulnerability, irritability

Sitting on the edge of the tub, as I flossed my teeth, my thoughts unravelled. Soon, everything would change: my daily routines, my sleeping patterns, my diet. I would eat a bagel for supper while watching TV. I'd let Molly sleep with me. I'd come home most days with shopping bags to fill the hole in my heart. I'd keep the radio on, even while I was away at work, to conceal the cold silence when I'd come through the door.

Steve would become even harder to access. He would enter a world I would never truly understand. He would experience war and the effects of poverty and hatred. It would plague his soul, without giving him any time to process or cope. For six months, our relationship would be put on hold. It would be tested, that's for sure, but it would not grow. We would grow separately and alone.

"Celebrate the signs of positive growth for both you and your partner." Soon I would have to tell him about the leaky roof, the higher tax bill, my grandfather's death, and his aunt's cancer, all on the phone, during our fifteen-minute weekly call.

"Try to be as positive as possible in your communications. Don't just share the problems, but the good news too."

The delay in the satellite phone would infuriate me: I would speak too fast and we would speak over each other, wasting valuable time. The distance between us would deepen with the echo of our voices over the faulty phone lines. I'd hold my tears, trying to be strong for him. He has enough to worry about, I'd tell myself. I would monitor my watch carefully to try to fit it all in. Sticky notes sat by the phone with the items I didn't want to forget. Time and time again, we would be cut off, for no reason. Those days would be bad. There was no closure, just questions. Even worse were the times I missed his call entirely and heard his voice broken and stuttering, on the answering machine.

"Missing a call always causes disappointments that are easily avoidable. Pre-arrange how many and the best times to phone to make the most of your call." I knew it could be another week before we spoke again. This was especially true when the units were deployed in the field. Away from the usual routes, he couldn't tell me where he'd be going, what he was doing, or when he'd be back on base.

"It's protocol," he assured me. "We can't take any chances, the phones could be monitored."

I would sit on the couch, looking out the large front window, and wait impatiently for the small black handset to ring, willing it to ring. Demanding that it ring. Often, it rang at two or three in the morning. I'd forget all about the sticky notes.

"It's a good idea to confirm the time of your call by email the day before."

The loneliness was difficult to express to the women I worked with at school. They revealed how they wished their spouse would leave for more than a week's fishing or hunting. They complained about their husbands over lunch and then went home to them every night. I ate my lunch quickly and went back to my classroom because sometimes being alone was better than being with a lunchroom full of civilians.

Countdown. Five more days until Phase Two began. I crawled into bed and spooned Steve. The lights were out and he was facing his usual side. He took my hands and wrapped them tightly around his body. We lay there for a while in silence, both thinking of what was to come. We put aside the hurtful words and the difficult roles that were ahead of us. Molly, already breaking the rules, sprawled at the foot of the bed. Steve turned around and faced me. He kissed my forehead, my cheeks. He put his lips on mine. We fell asleep wrapped together.

Meanwhile, the clerks at CFB Petawawa were in building G-101. They were sealing the envelopes holding the military-issued handbooks, describing Phase Two. I had been there before. I'd already gotten my copy.

3 | Variable Duration

"More than 2,900 Canadian soldiers, sailors, and Air Force personnel are deployed overseas on operational missions. On any given day, about 8,000 Canadian Forces members—one-third of our deployable force—are preparing for, engaged in, or returning from an overseas mission." — www.familyforce.ca

The unimaginable can happen on a day like any other, a gash ripping through the fabric of ordinary life. On this day, the sun shone, not a cloud in the sky. The morning started like all the others: a bowl of Cheerios, a large decaf double-double, and a five-minute drive to the school where I taught.

Teaching Gr. 4/5 split classes always had me running for something. Roxanne, one of my grade five students, needed her work printed on blue paper. She had problems with her vision, and the coloured paper made it easier for her read. Shortly after morning announcements, I darted out of my classroom to make the copy before she noticed I'd forgotten. The aroma of strong coffee wafted from the teacher's lounge at the end of the hall, where I was headed. I breathed it in deeply; it would be a while before I could have it again.

"Hi, Pauline. You on prep?"

"Yeah. Listen. Did you hear what happened?" Pauline asked, moving in closer to me. She always had a secret to share, usually about someone else—that so-and-so might soon be going on stress leave or that so-and-so was hoarding all the art supplies. I usually kept my distance.

"Hear what?" I asked with a shudder as I caught sight of the worry in her eyes. Was it another death, a roadside bomb, what? At General Lake

Public School, almost all the kids, and some teachers, too, were military.

"Two planes just crashed into some government buildings in the U.S. I was in the office when Jim got the call."

"What the hell?"

"I know."

"How did this happen?"

"Nobody knows." We both stood there, staring at the coffee maker as it finished dripping into the glass pot, making a hush sound. The secretary's voice on the school intercom snapped us out of our silence.

"Just a reminder that the choir is meeting in the library during morning recess. Please do not linger in the halls, and be on time. Thank you."

"I have to get back to class," I said. Our eyes met as I turned to leave. She was no longer married to Patrick, who had been discharged from the army, but she still worried just as much. Some things you can't divorce. I headed back to my classroom with my hands snuggled against my stomach. I was grateful our baby wasn't born yet. Just the size of a peanut and safe inside her mama.

September 11, 2001, was one of the longest days of my teaching career. Yard duty felt like a war zone.

"Curtis, Brayden, stop! That's enough!" I managed to get to them before there was blood. Dishevelled hair and collars stretched out, hanging loosely around their necks. Curtis was close to tears as I approached them on the edge of the baseball field.

"He started this time! He called my dad a wog," said Brayden pointing to his adversary.

"Did not. I called him a fat wog," said Curtis, smirking through his braces.

"Seriously? Both of you, get to the office now and keep your hands off of each other."

Most of the older students went home for lunch. They had seen the footage on TV. They came back wired, joking about the end of the world. Teachers in the younger grades hadn't talked to their students about what had happened in New York City that morning; they still hadn't made sense of it themselves. But that didn't stop the kids from hurtling their bodies into each other all day long. They could feel the restlessness, the anxiety. I raced from one shoving match to another, checking my watch in between clashes, counting the minutes for the bell to ring. I gave up on making them stand at attention like soldiers in proper rows before they entered the school, instead waving them inside like a herd of cows. It was 2:20 in the afternoon and I was ready to go home. We were all unravelling.

Molly greeted me with her long, feathered wagging tail. I let her out and immediately turned on the television. To my complete horror, I watched people throwing themselves out of a burning building and falling to their deaths, like stuntmen in a disaster movie. The scenes just couldn't be real. Others were covered in white dust, crying into the camera and begging for help to find their family members. Names written on signs and photos squeezed in hands, desperately shared on TV. I sat down on the edge of the coffee table and covered my mouth with both hands. The images played and replayed all through the night. The world had changed. I knew it would never be the same.

Molly jumped up on the sofa and laid her head on my lap. Steve was still in Bosnia. He'd been there six months already—now it was an extended tour. Steve's higher rank meant more responsibility and an extra month apart. The end of the rotation was always the worst: so close, yet too far away. You just held your breath until the plane landed on Canadian soil. Only then did you allow yourself some relief. Now, in the shadow of the collapsing Twin Towers, the home stretch became unbearable. I worried constantly about Steve's safety. I had no one to tell me everything would be all right, to help calm my hormonal nerves. No one to reassure me there was still good in the world and that bringing a baby into it was not a selfish act. My closest family—my mom and two younger brothers—were 400 kilometres away, and my mom had her own kindergarten class to take care of. I was on my own, growing a child inside me, while the world was going to shit and my husband was in the middle of it. And I couldn't even have a drink.

I reached for the phone and called Alice. She had been my closest friend for the past three years. She was a transplant, too, and a fellow teacher at the same school on base. Her husband, Rick, was in Steve's unit for a while.

"Can you believe this?" she said. "What the hell is happening?"

"I don't know." I rested my hands on my belly, wondering when I would start to show.

"Are you okay? Do you want to come over? I don't think you should be alone right now," she said. Alice was home on maternity leave with her daughter. Work wasn't the same without her. She had always been such a comfort, especially when one of us got a crazy letter from a deranged parent, which was often.

"I want to stay home, just in case—"

"He probably won't call, Dan. I'm sure the phones are all shut down."

"I know, but I wouldn't want to miss it if ..."

"Okay, well, call me if you need anything. I'll send Rick over to get you."

"No worries. I'll be fine."

"I'll call you tomorrow. But promise me you'll call us back if you need anything. Don't be a hero over there."

I became obsessed with CNN. I followed families as they searched for their lost loved ones—a sponge for all the suffering that was happening in our northern hemisphere. I could relate to the unknown. I knew what it was like to worry and hope for the best, to push away the worst-case scenario from your mind, to wake up in the middle of the night from a terrible dream and pray to God that it was not a premonition and just the fear growing with the darkness. Witnessing their grief gave my nights purpose as I counted down the sleeps until Steve returned home.

Work was a welcome routine. My students were dealing with the catastrophe of the terrorist attack, too. A third of them were affected, as I was, by this latest deployment. They were left without a mom or dad—or in one case, both parents, even the stepfather; the ten-year-old boy had to stay with his grandmother. I needed to show up every day for these kids, who were familiar with war and bombs and death. Our safety nets were flawed; our closest family members served country before family. In those days after 9/11, our classroom became the one thing we could count on.

I checked my email often. I staggered between faking it beautifully and collapsing into full-blown anguish while I waited to hear from Steve.

To tame my nerves, I took Molly for a walk every night up and down the large hill behind the house. I believed Steve was safe because I would have heard otherwise. No news is good news in the army. Still, I needed reassurance. I needed comforting. I needed to know I was not alone in this big, bad, self-destructing world.

On the fifth day, the phone rang. I knew it was him because of the delay on the phone after I answered.

"Dan, it's me."

"Jesus, how are you?"

"I'm fine, everything's fine. They shut everything down after what happened. I couldn't call, but I wanted to."

"God, it's so good to hear your voice," I said, tears stinging my eyes.

"I'm so sorry I couldn't call sooner. How are you? How's the baby?"

"Fine, we're fine. Can you believe what happened?"

"No. I can't," he said it in a way that made me abruptly change the subject. I already suspected that this act of war would mean more time away, and I couldn't go there right now.

"Are you still on schedule to come home on October 10? Is that still happening?"

"Yeah, still on schedule."

"I just want you home."

"I know. Listen, I should go, there's a huge lineup of guys waiting to use the phone."

"Already?" I said, wiping my nose with my sleeve. "Try to call back soon and please stay safe."

"I will. I love you, babe. We're almost there."

"Me, too," I said, barely able to get it out. The stress from the week finally hit me in one hard whack. I could finally let go. I hung up the phone and the tears fell hard and fast. I gave in. I dropped onto the couch and forced my face into the cushion. This heartache was too much for Molly, who deserted me as I made space for the pain. I flipped onto my back and tried to breathe in deeply, feeling guilty for giving in to the darkness. I rubbed my belly. I'm sorry, little one.

Just a few months before, I'd flown to Paris to meet Steve for his three-week leave in July. We hadn't seen each other in almost four months. The whole trip was out of character for us. We were both the type who made lists for everything; things to pack, people to call, things to buy, bills to pay. But on this trip, there were no lists, just day after spontaneous, unplanned day. We were so lucky his leave landed during my summer holiday—this kind of good fortune was rare in military life. But now somebody else was at the bottom of the totem pole. After a few nights in Paris, we jumped from train to train and visited Florence, Venice, and Barcelona, all on a whim with our backpacks and EuroRail passes. We picked a city on our map and just went, not bothering with hotel reservations, even during the busiest month of the year. Somehow, it all worked out. We were never without a place to sleep. Late dinners, litres of wine, walks on the cobblestone streets, hand in hand. We were so carefree. And together for eighteen consecutive nights.

We made love more on this trip then we had all year long. I felt like a different woman when I arrived in Paris, a more sensual and sexy version of myself. I left the conservative teacher at home and let the adventurous, amorous woman out. Every barrier I had ever raised between us was dismantled on that continent, including the Catholic girl I carried around deep inside. I was intoxicated by Europe, and for once in our lives together, time did not seem to matter.

And now I missed his skin so much, the way it felt against mine. I wanted him to hold me until I fell asleep in his arms. Instead, I lay on the couch, frantic images blinking on the TV, and tried to figure out which city our baby had been conceived in.

Steve returned home after seven months in Bosnia. I picked him up from 3RCR (the third Royal Canadian Regiment), the building where he worked, on the night of October 10, right on schedule. This reunion was sweeter than the others. The last time we had been together was our vacation. Molly was the one who was with me when I took the pregnancy test. Steve loved me more than he did before—I could tell. He was afraid to hurt the baby when we made love that night. He was gentle. Our unborn child was already bonding us together in a way we hadn't experienced before. He rubbed my belly and talked to the baby with his face squished up against my stomach. We were finally becoming a family after being married four years, a unit of three plus a German shepherd.

On the seventh day after his return, as I walked down the hall at school, I felt my lower abdomen cramp. It was already past two in the afternoon. I decided to wait for the 3:00 bell. Then I drove myself to emergency. I called Steve and asked him to meet me there.

"I'm at the hospital," I said trying to steady my voice.

"What happened?"

"I've had some cramping and I have a bad feeling—"

"I'll meet you there babe."

"Hurry," I said.

I knew from the look on the technician's face that something was not right. She showed me the amniotic sac where the baby should have been. She pointed to the screen. A dark fuzzy circle, empty. Our baby had vanished and no one could tell us why.

That night, we cried. Everyone we knew was pregnant, but our child would not be born. Our hopes and dreams for our little family were shattered. The box of children's books I'd been collecting for years would remain closed and unread. Steve held me tenderly as I damned the gods for their unjust punishment. The ache I felt in my body was unbearable; the emptiness ricocheted inside me until I ran out of tears and numbness crept over me like the blackest, thickest night. For twelve hours, we grieved together. For that one night, at least, our pain was the same.

Steve quickly moved on. He worked long hours and often volunteered for courses that took him away from home. But I couldn't stop the tears.

"Dan, you need to get busy again. It helps, trust me."

"I can't just forget like you. I actually feel stuff. I'm not a machine." I started to resent his ability to bounce back. Something still pressed hard against me.

I went back to work a week later, and I did my best, but my spark was gone. I was a robot spewing out curriculum. And by the time I got home, I just wanted to sleep. It took every ounce of energy to pretend all day long, to give what I didn't have. I couldn't get the dark fuzzy circle out of my head; it was etched inside me like a fossil.

A few days after the ultrasound, I was admitted for a D&C, a surgical procedure to clear the tissue from inside my uterus. Steve dropped me off and went to work. It was only day surgery, after all. Even so, I was terrified as they put me under. They were about to suck the last bit of my pregnancy away and I was not ready to let it go. I sat up in my paper blue gown and pleaded with the three nurses.

"Please don't do this. I don't want you to do this." I squeezed my stomach as they prepared to shave my pubic hair. A nurse with frizzy blond hair and the roundest blue eyes moved into my sight, directly under the light.

"Just lie down, dear. You won't feel a thing," she said. "This procedure will help you get pregnant again. It cleans everything out, like spring cleaning. You'll have many more babies after this." She tucked my hair back into my cap, like she was my fairy godmother. All she was missing was the wand.

I woke up an hour later to an empty room. Another nurse came in and took my blood pressure.

"So, how far along were you, hon?" she asked.

"Fourteen weeks," I said, almost in a whisper.

"Just long enough to get used to it, eh, and tell everyone about it, I'm sure? Oh hon, you'll have six more someday, you'll see."

I was one month away from turning twenty-seven when I lost my first baby. I knew I would have been a great mom. Steve and I were so ready to become parents. We both had good jobs. We had a home, a yard to play in. Instead, I had to continue to be a pseudo-parent for my students, and this was just not enough anymore. I started to judge the bad parenting I witnessed: the thoughtless lunches and the parents who were always unplugged from their kids' education. I couldn't bear to see young parents pushing a stroller, especially the teenage ones who smoked beside their babies. Seeing this would send me into a seething rage. Even being around friends with kids was intolerable. I started to withdraw from the world around me. Steve put up with it for a while, until he couldn't anymore.

"You seriously need to move on from this," he said. He'd just come home from another week in the field. It had been almost three months since we lost the baby.

"I'm trying Steve, I really am."

"I've been patient, Dan. Get yourself sorted out. I can't deal with your negativity anymore."

"I can't help it. I don't want to be sad," I cried.

"Fix it," he said.

I started seeing a counsellor in January. Her name was Dorothy and she wasn't that much older than me. She was kind, but she wasn't married and she didn't have children. How could she understand what I was going through?

"I recognize the five stages of grieving. I know I have to go through them all to move on and that it takes time. I'm just really impatient," I joked. She wrote everything down as I said it, word for word. It drove me crazy, but I was not bold enough to tell her so. She would smile as I spoke and often said that I was "so together" and that she looked forward to my visits.

"We could have been great friends, Danielle, if we'd met another way. It's really too bad."

Dorothy told me that we often accumulate difficult experiences if we don't deal with them. I was just having a hard time getting back up from these collective hardships, she said.

"You can spend your whole life just trying to get over your childhood," she said. "Never mind what happens after. Nobody is shatterproof. This will take more time."

But time wasn't making anything better.

On a Friday in February, Steve walked through the door after five nights in the field, wearing his army fatigues and carrying his big green duffle bag over his shoulder. We had spoken once that week, but it wasn't for long. I could tell he was disappointed that I was still sounding so down.

"Hey, I'm home. I'm going to jump in the shower."

"Okay. How was the rest of your week?" I hollered from the kitchen.

"Hard. It's so freaking cold at night. I packed a little too light this time. I'll see you in a bit."

"Okay. Just getting supper ready." I kept my voice perky. I wanted us to have a good weekend, since they were all we had.

"So what do you want to do tonight?" he asked after his shower. His long, wet lashes were still stuck together, like little stars, and he'd wrapped a navy towel tightly around his waist. He could have easily been featured in a Gillette commercial. He was too handsome, the kind that caused heartache. The kind that always made you worry: tall, dark, muscular, with the most beautiful smile.

"I don't know, really. It was a rough week at school. The kids were wild with the snow and all."

"Well, do you want to go see a movie or something?"

"Maybe. But I think I might just want to stay home."

All hope for the night drained from his voice. "Okay, Dan, this has seriously got to stop."

"What?" I asked, sucking in my breath and holding it.

"I'm done with you being all miserable and shit. It's such a downer to come home to a depressed wife after being gone all week. Go outside, get some exercise. You're not the first woman to ever have a miscarriage. You need to get over it!"

"There he goes again: Mr. Sensitive. I swear you're an even bigger ass every time you come back from the field. Are you sure they don't serve you asshole in those ration packs?"

He shook his head and walked away, as usual. I left supper on the counter and went to bed hungry while he watched TV and surfed the Web. I tried to read but I couldn't get through a single page. I hated everything about the army when I fell asleep that night. Everything.

When I woke up, he was already out of bed, an early riser even on weekends.

"Steve, can we talk for a minute?"

"Only a minute. I'm heading to the gym, so make it fast."

"Jesus. Yes, sir," I snapped.

"Okay. You know what? I'm done talking. Get some drugs or I'm out of here! You have a choice to make."

Steve came to the doctor's appointment with me. My doctor knew how I felt about taking drugs; we'd already discussed it weeks before. I was afraid I would become dependent, a fear that had been passed down through my family like my curly hair. After I lost the baby and continued to feel depressed, he had recommended some books: *Conversations with God*, books 1 through 3, and *The Celestine Prophecy*, to start. He wasn't an average doctor. When he first suggested taking antidepressants to help me get over the hump, I refused.

"You wear glasses, don't you?" he asked. "Some people need glasses, Danielle, others don't. You need glasses." But I wasn't ready then.

The three of us sat quietly while Steve explained that he could no longer deal with my depression. "You need to fix it, Doc. It's seriously affecting me and my job. I have a lot of responsibility as a master corporal, and this has to end today." The doctor looked at me. I couldn't say a word. I sank deeper into the chair.

"Do you want this medication, Danielle?" I nodded, my eyes watering.

"Well, it looks like your problem will soon be fixed, Steve," he said, standing up and patting him on the shoulder. I continued to look at my feet as my doctor strained to make eye contact with me.

"I'm counting on it," Steve said.

I sat there like a little girl, hands tucked in my lap, scolded for being too sad for too long. The hardcore feminist who had once co-founded the Women's Studies Student Association at the University of Ottawa a few years before was barely recognizable. It was as if that part of me had stepped outside my body and disappeared out that office door.

Slowly, the dark haze began to lift. The sorrow was still there but the medication made me more tolerable, at least to Steve.

Our loss hadn't brought us closer together. Sure, for a brief moment, we were united in our heartbreak, but, in the end, the space between us grew like a night's fog, heavy, thick, and impassable. No matter how much I wanted to see past it, I couldn't.

Florence: that's where our baby was conceived. We would have named her Gabrielle, after a street we loved in Venice, when we were both smiling and holding hands.

When time had stood still for us.

4 | Yellow Ribbons

The yellow ribbon is worn by a "woman of destiny [who is under a test or trial as she waits for her beloved to return. Will she be true to him?" — "Yellow Ribbon" entry, History and Etymology, Early Puritan, Wikipedia

The grey skies hung in contrast to the lemon-coloured ribbons that bobbed on the backs of cars and glowed in the windows of local businesses; they fluttered from posts and snow-filled trees that lined the highway. On the road from Petawawa to Pembroke, the message boards of twenty-seven car dealerships welcomed back Roto 0: the first official rotation to Kabul. In less than ten days, soldiers would be driving their brand-new vehicles off the lots, bought and paid for with their tax-free danger pay. It was February 2004. The soldiers had been gone for six long months.

Twelve days after my emergency C-section, Steve devoted himself to a three-month leadership course in Gagetown, before the Afghanistan mission. He was on the fast track to moving up the ranks.

"Can't you put this one off until next year?" I asked, struggling to nurse the baby, his weight bearing down on my stitches.

"Not if I want to get promoted," he said, lacing up his boots. "They only run it so often. Don't you think it's better I leave now, when Owen won't even notice I'm gone? Better now than when he's one or two."

"Guess so." Nothing I could say would change his mind.

"I'm doing this for the family," he said.

"But what if I can't do this alone? I've never had a baby before."

"Isn't that what a mother's instincts are for?"

"I've got no one here, Steve, and—"

"You have Alice, she's done this before, and there's the family resource centre," Steve said.

The cold air lingered long after he closed the door. The hollow in my chest was so deep, I could barely stay upright as I nursed and changed my son.

Two days after Steve left for the East coast, still recovering from the surgery and learning quickly how to be a single mother, I lugged our cat to the vet. Baby carrier in one hand and animal carrier in the other, at a time when I wasn't supposed to carry anything.

"Just take him," I said to the young woman at the desk. The cat suffered from a rare form of multiple sclerosis. He was only four, but could no longer make it to the litter box. Steve had offered to take him in and get him euthanized, like the vet had suggested months ago, but I wouldn't let him. I couldn't sentence him to his death while my child was growing within me.

"I'm sorry it's taken me so long," I cried.

"What about the cat carrier?" asked the veteran's assistant.

"Keep it," I sobbed.

My stitches split open that week and got infected. Thank God for antibiotics. There was no time for rest: Owen's colic was starting.

Steve visited us once from Gagetown. He'd driven from the East Coast to Petawawa with three other guys, twelve straight hours on the road, but he could stay only one night—they had to report in by Monday morning. Steve was sick with a hideous cold and so was Owen. I spent the night in the bathroom with the steamer on full blast to help Owen breathe, and thought of a story I'd heard about Inuit women who sucked the snot out of their babies' noses when they were sick. I contemplated waking Steve and making him suck Owen's snot out. Instead, I sat on the black and white tiled floor, listening to my husband's snores.

After the leadership course, Steve stayed home long enough to help us move into our new house in Pembroke. We unpacked every single box in less than twenty-four hours. We hadn't been planning to move, but our neighbours had wanted to buy our home to make into a guest house adjacent to their newly renovated farmhouse. They made us an offer we couldn't refuse, and we found another house, a Cape Cod-style home on the outskirts of town. It was farther away from the base and surrounded by mature trees.

A month later, he left for Afghanistan on the six-month tour. I was diligent about sending him photos through email and tucked into the care packages I made to keep him up to date on Owen's development. I captured Owen's first year in five scrapbooks, to ensure Steve wouldn't miss a thing. I kept it all together, and I was still standing.

Then, before I knew it, the year was over and Steve was coming back—really coming back. One thing was for sure, having a baby to care for made the time go by faster than being alone. But it wasn't any easier. I cherished the time I had with my sweet baby boy. I was lucky to have a whole year of maternity leave. It was, however, bittersweet without his dad. I wrote to the school board, asking for two days of paid leave to spend with my husband and son. I needed a couple of days to ease Steve into the routine of fatherhood. Patrolling the streets of Kabul was one thing; taking care of our thirteen-month-old son was a whole other operation. My letter was solid.

"What do you think?" I asked Alice before submitting it.

"If they say no, they're the heartless bastards I think they are," she answered. "Seriously Dan, it made me cry. There's no way they can refuse this."

Request denied. One day unpaid only. Wouldn't want to set a precedent. I should have lied and called in sick.

"Wouldn't want to actually support military families even though they say they do," I fumed to Alice.

"The people who make these decisions have no clue in hell what we go through! How can they when they go home to their own families every night?" she said.

We were driving past the school board office. I flipped them the bird.

"That's pretty mature," she said.

"I know. But it's driving me crazy. I can't help myself."

"Some people will never grasp what we give up so they can sleep tight every night. Don't let them defeat you."

I laughed. "Okay, Zen master," I said.

"Not long now, eh, Danielle?" It was Greg, the custodian. The radio was on as usual, a local country station. Greg listened all day long, keeping me up to date on the Afghanistan mission, even during my news fasts. He saw the load of marking I'd done on the weekend and waved me on.

I opened the door to my classroom and hurried to the front, dropping into my chair to take the first sip of my coffee. It was 8:10 am. I had forty-five minutes to get myself ready. As a teacher, I'd always prided myself on being ready the day before, with all the handouts photocopied and my pages bristling with sticky notes. In the last few weeks, though, I'd barely kept one step ahead of the kids. As I rifled through the bags looking for my math exercise books, I felt a jab in my belly again, this one tinged with fear. Would Steve really understand the last email I had sent? I'd written it late at night, three days ago, after yet another strained phone call. It seemed we were running out of things to talk about, even though we spoke only fifteen minutes a week.

"Well, anything new over there?" I asked.

"Nothing, Dan. It's hot and dirty and I can't wait to get back."

"I'm sure."

"You? I mean, what's new in Pembroke?"

"Nothing. Nothing's ever new in Pembroke," I said.

"Right. Well, it's better than being in this filthy place."

"I don't doubt that." I paused. "Well, Owen should be waking up soon."

"Make sure you tell him his daddy misses him."

"I will."

"Not much longer, Dan. I know it's getting old. We're in the home stretch."

"Stay safe. We're counting down with you."

"Love you, babe."

This often happened to us at the end of a tour. You start to believe, that if you rush through the conversation, you will be that much closer to being together in the flesh. But after a few of those truncated conversations in the last month, and spending most of the year by myself with our infant son, I was desperate to tell him what I was really feeling. I was exhausted: from worrying, from doing it all alone, and from agonizing about the next time he would go away. I had definitely reached my number. Four tours in fewer than eight years. I couldn't pretend any more as we talked over the satellite phone with the delay making our separation palpable. He left me for nine months with a newborn. I was done sucking it up. I no longer had the energy to explain to him how much Owen was growing and changing every day. I resented being alone and I begrudged him, despite the pride I felt for what he was doing. I knew Steve was making a difference in Afghanistan, but somehow, that was no longer enough. Not even close.

"What's with you today?" Alice asked when I met her in the hall.

"Nothing. Same as always," I said.

"He's still coming home next Wednesday, right?"

"Yup. I'm not going to sleep till he gets his ass home."

"Why don't you and Owen come over for dinner tonight? Rick's in the field for a couple of days. It's just me and the kids. It'll do you some good to eat with someone."

"I'm not alone. I have Owen."

"Sure you do, but I mean grown-up talk. Don't isolate yourself. Don't forget I have the T-shirt too—three of them and counting."

"Right. The men get medals and we get T-shirts, wrinkles, and grey hair. How's that fair?"

"Come over. We'll put a pizza in the oven and make a salad. Okay?"

"Sounds good."

At least one other person on staff knew the reunion wouldn't be all ice cream and cherries. It wasn't anything like what they depicted on the news with the tacky music and hugs all around. A few other military spouses taught at the school, but none of them were infantry wives. Their husbands weren't gone as much as Steve and Rick. Only Alice knew how much time I spent alone. They called us field widows for a reason.

I pulled into Alice's driveway, which looked like it had been cut out of a snow block. I was getting sick of plowing mine with our 4-wheeler after I put Owen to sleep. It was only February; the snow would fall for a long while yet. Alice's husband was exempt from this tour because he'd just had knee surgery. He wasn't happy about it: no one wants to be the guy left behind. And he was missing out on the danger pay, which would have financed the garage he wanted to build. In the months Steve was away, he'd recovered enough to go on a three-day training exercise. I wondered what kind of injury it would take to keep Steve home.

"Look who's here you guys, it's Danielle and Owen!"

Alice's kids stood at the top of the stairs waiting for us to take off our boots and jackets. Her daughter was three and her son was only twelve months.

"Come on in, supper's in the oven. Give me the little guy." I handed him off, still in his snowsuit, hat, and mitts. "This kid's a giant! Steve is going to be shocked when he sees how much he's grown."

"I know. They miss a lot, don't they?" ·

"More than they'll ever know," she said, wrinkling her brow.

"Do you think if they did, if they really did know how much they missed, they would still choose to go?" I said hanging up my jacket.

"Well, we all know that at least half of them are told to go, but the other half I think would be split down the middle. One half would probably stay, but the other half would still be lining up. We all know who those guys are," added Alice, quickly covering her mouth with her hand. "I'm sorry, I didn't mean it that way."

"I know," I said.

"It's not a bad thing, it's an honourable thing. We need people who are loyal to the cause," she said, sitting Owen in front of the heap of toys in the living room.

"It just sucks when that person is your husband and he was born with DNA that predisposes him to being the poster boy for the goddamn army."

"I invited you over to take your mind off things, not to stress you out," she reminded me.

"It's okay. You're right, Steve would volunteer to go. He's that guy. That's why I sent him an email a few days ago. But I still haven't heard anything from him yet."

"What did you say?"

"It was the email, Alice. The one you should never send to your husband overseas."

"Holy shit, Dan, not a Dear John letter?"

"No, the other one. The one that says I'm so sick and tired of being sick and tired, and when will this come to an end?"

"Oh. That one. What do you think he'll say?"

I knew exactly what he'd say. The part I wasn't sure about was what I was going to do about it. I could have answered the email myself. I'd known him eleven years and I was sure Afghanistan hadn't changed him that much.

"He'd tell me that I knew when I married him that he was in the military. That it's what he loves; that he's worked too hard to get to where he is to quit now. He'd say it's all he knows and he's good at it, not to mention that he's serving his country. And he'd say that, if I'm too weak to be an army wife, I know where the door is. He hates ultimatums. He'd tell me to just do what I have to do."

"That's a little harsh," Alice said, twisting the wedding ring on her finger.

"That's my reality. You know him. He's a lifer. It's up to me to be the bad guy if I want things to change."

"Well, maybe this time will be different. If anything can transform a person, it's a baby."

"I don't know. I hope to God a shift has happened, because I'm tired of living life alone, of raising a child on my own."

"I know it's not easy, but doesn't teaching keep your mind off things? At least we have jobs. I can't imagine how all the wives cope who stay home all day."

"Teaching used to be enough. Not anymore. It's not just the tours. What about all the training: weeks—no, months—in the field? That will never change. The part that completely sucks is that I still love him so much, Alice."

Silence filled the room. Even the kids were still.

"I think I've finally reached a point where I believe I deserve to be happy and supported, too. He's not the only one with goals and dreams, you know! I'm sorry, I'm getting so worked up."

"It's okay, I get it. You need to let it out."

"It's just … everything's on hold when he's gone. I feel so guilty every time I leave Owen with a sitter since he's already with one all day when I'm at work. And there will always be another course, another tour, and another situation where the army needs Steve and only Steve because of his bleeping qualifications. They brainwash them, Alice. They make it seem like he's the *only* guy for the job and that if he doesn't do it, he's letting down the whole country! Enough already. When will he realize that he's just being used? And the cost is his family."

"I swear they put something in their food," she said.

"It wouldn't surprise me one bit," I said. "Can you believe *The National* wants to film our reunion? They called me last week. It's one thing to get footage of Steve in Afghanistan and me at home with Owen—that, I agreed to—but now they want to end it with the perfect Hallmark moment by sticking a camera in our faces after six months apart. Seriously?"

"What did you say?"

"I said no. Hell no! And Steve agreed. He said he doesn't want to be on national news either after being on a stupid plane for two days."

"Those freaking people need to spend a year with us to see what it's really about. If only it was just one happy reunion after another."

"Exactly. They're not getting their two-minute feel-good segment from this family. Go find another sucker."

Email inbox: three. My heart thumped so hard that my hands shook. I clicked the inbox, scanning for his email. It wasn't there. Nothing but junk mail. I turned off the computer and went straight to bed. I was too tired to feel anything.

The next morning I woke up before Owen and hurried downstairs to the computer without even making coffee. I slumped myself over the black swivel chair and tapped impatiently on the desk as it booted up.

And there it was. Inbox: Steve Daniel. A wave of nausea made me feel as though I might pass out. Would this just all blow up in my face?

> Dan,
> I read your email, and I just can't get into this right
> now. You could have waited until I got back to discuss
> this. I'll be home in just over a week.
> Steve

I stared at the screen. Rage rose from my feet to my forehead. Three measly sentences? He always managed to make me feel unreasonable when I was at my breaking point. Asshole. Ass-hole! It doesn't matter how I feel, he will always do what he wants. His dreams. His needs. His agenda. I could no longer live this way.

On cue, Owen started to wail.

"Another day," I whispered to myself, hot tears spilling down my cheeks as I ran up the stairs three at a time to get Owen ready for the day. I kissed his cheeks and did what I did every day, but this time, my wretchedness was caked with anger, which I had never allowed myself to express around my son. I wanted to curl up in bed and pull the blankets over my head. I wanted to yell at everyone who asked how I was: Do you *really* want to know? I'm worried out of my mind that my husband will come home in a body bag and that my son will grow up without a father. I don't want to pretend for one more day, not even one more minute.

At school, I got out of the van and slammed the door. I wanted to rip off the magnetic yellow ribbon stuck on my door and toss it into traffic.

"Good morning, Danielle, how are you?"

I glared at my VP and smiled. "Fine," I said. "I'm just fine."

Pick up son: check. Supper: check. Laundry: check. Bath time: check. Schoolwork: check. I was making it through my day, but I was cracking, the way a drinking glass eventually does after too many cycles in the dishwasher. The glass is cracked but it still holds milk. You know it's going to break soon, but you keep using it until it falls apart, in pieces.

I woke up and looked at the clock. 5:30. Owen was still sleeping, thank God. Steve would be coming home the next day. I wondered where he was at that moment. He had already left Afghanistan—it took two days to get home. Maybe he was in Germany, Dubai, Timbuctoo. Wherever he was, he was decompressing, unable to give me his location, which was code for ridiculously drunk and stupid. This was the army's way of getting the guys ready to come home to their families.

I sat at the kitchen table with a cup of hot coffee in my hands and thought of how Smitty's wife must be feeling. He'd been killed in a Bombardier Iltis; by a roadside bomb only one month after the men had arrived in Afghanistan. Two soldiers had died in that explosion, both from Base Petawawa. Steve had to go out and patrol the following day in the same unprotected jeep, near an area where Smitty had been killed. Steve had missed the ramp ceremony and didn't get a chance to say good-bye. He didn't want to talk about it when he called home. His trailer was across from Smitty's; they had spoken the morning before he was killed. And Smitty's wife, waiting like me, for the rest of them to come home. Except that her husband would never come home to her again. I wondered if she would live in a perpetual dream, hoping he would show up one day on her doorstep.

I counted my blessings then, despite my beaten heart. Others were hurting much more than me. I held gratitude in my heart for keeping my husband safe. Owen still had his daddy.

The next day, I drank a whole pot of coffee at school after my usual large double-double. Alice came to visit me during the final recess, knowing I would be bouncing off the walls.

"Well, hello there, Madame Fraser, how are you holding up?"

"I'm going mental! I don't know how I'm going to get through the next couple hours."

"After nine months apart this year, I'm sure you can wait until 8:30 tonight."

"Funny one."

"Did you sleep last night?"

"Barely."

"You should have gotten drunk. I could've come over."

"I did manage three glasses of wine. It goes down pretty fast while you're mopping the floors."

"Good for you. A little buzz doesn't hurt while you're housecleaning," she said with a wink. "So, have you decided what you'll wear tonight?"

"My baby-blue fitted turtleneck."

"Sweet. Up or down?"

"Down and curly."

"Sounds perfect to me. Steve will have his hands all over you before you even get in the door."

"We'll see … it feels like forever this time. Really. Forever."

"You guys will find your groove again. Give it a couple of days. You're strong, Dan."

"I hope so."

"You just need to shut out the rest of the world right now. Are his parents coming up?"

"Not for at least a couple of weeks. I spoke to them last night."

"Lucky you. I swear, Greg's parents would sleep right between us if they could. They never give us space when he gets back. They'd be at the building waiting with me. Be happy that it'll just be you and Owen, and no national news."

I could barely eat supper. Of course, Owen was unaware of the big event, though he would repeat after me, "Daddy soon, daddy soon." I had celebrated his first birthday the month before, making up for Steve's absence by inviting every mother and baby I knew. Twelve babies on one couch made for an interesting first-birthday photo. I was so excited for my two boys to see each other again.

I washed and dried the dishes and put them away. I usually let them dry in the rack, but I needed to stay busy. While Owen played in his playpen, I brushed my teeth and changed into my blue turtleneck. I flipped my hair over and sprayed it lightly with hairspray. Next, the cherry lip gloss and the perfume Steve had bought for me in England when he did the Cambrian Patrol—he'd brought home a silver medal that time. I checked myself out in the mirror, fluffing my hair and turning around to check out my butt in my jeans. I hadn't lost all the baby weight I'd planned to while Steve was gone. Would he be disappointed when he saw me?

"Okay, buddy, it's show time," I said, bundling up Owen. "Let's go pick up Daddy."

"Daddy soon," he replied.

"Yes. Owen, Daddy soon."

I strapped him into his car seat and wiped the snow off the windshield with my bare hand. I blasted the heat and buckled myself in, turning the radio to CBC. A male commentator began to list his numerous reasons for Canada's unnecessary role in Afghanistan. I flicked it off, inhaled deeply, and breathed out slowly as I backed out onto the road.

As I pulled up to the intersection right before the base, I saw a tank sitting in the snow along with a lighted sign that said Welcome Home Roto 0. Yellow ribbons flanked both sides of the intersection, flapping in the cold winter wind. It was 7:30 pm but, even so, there was a lot of traffic. Steve wouldn't arrive for another hour, but I was always early. There was no way I would be late for this. I pulled through the entrance under the sign All Visitors Must Check In. The gate was not supervised and displayed a perpetual green light. My heart fluttered and I took another deep breath, exhaling as I passed through.

I pulled into the Y-101 parking lot. "This is where Daddy works, Owen." The parking lot was still fairly empty. I parked close and got Owen out of his car seat.

"Okay, big boy, Daddy will be here soon."

"Daddy soon."

I heaved him into my arms and sheltered his face against the cold. Walking into the large cement building made me queasier than driving onto base. Soldiers wearing black boots and camouflage rushed around with clipboards. Privates and corporals were setting up tables with Tim Hortons coffee and Timbits, fruit juice and bottled water.

Other parents started to pile in, some with three kids wearing their pyjamas and anxiously awaiting their dads and moms. You could always tell who the newlyweds were: all done up and alone, staring into space blindly, very close to vomiting, and unsure how they made it through their first six months. I smiled at one of the girls. She was blond and very pretty. She smiled back meekly. I felt sorry for her, and then guilty. Even after my fourth tour, it wasn't any easier. She wore her yellow ribbon on her coat collar. I didn't bother pinning mine anymore. I didn't have to. The yellow ribbons were permanently wrapped around me, a tight corset.

I turned my attention to Owen, who was sitting in my lap and already falling asleep. "My little angel," I whispered. "Maybe we'll all sleep better once Daddy's home."

I looked at my watch. Thirty minutes to go.

"Oh, hi. Danielle, right?"

"Yes. You're Fitzpatrick's wife?"

"Shelly."

"We met at the Christmas mess dinner last year," I said.

"Yup, that was me. We were both pregnant then," she said.

"That's true. I was huge, with less than a month to go," I said. "You had a girl, right?"

"My third."

"Wow."

"I can't wait for those boys to finally get here. This one wasn't like the others."

"Nope," I said, shifting Owen's weight in my arms.

"So, have you heard about O'Malley and Bazinet? Their marriages didn't make it," she said.

"I did. The Hunters, too."

"I heard Hunter's wife ended up with a master corporal from the Qs."

"Geez. I hadn't heard that," I said.

"PMQ gossip, sadly. I think we'll see a lot more breakups after this rotation."

"You might be right," I said, biting down on my lower lip.

I looked towards the doors where people were still coming in. The energy in the building was not jovial, not full of excitement. It was heaviness mixed with trepidation and relief, cracked hearts and uncertain futures. As much as these wives looked composed with their perfectly coiffed hair and painted lips, I knew the truth. Afghanistan was a battle that had affected us all.

"They're here! They're here!" someone yelled from the other end of the hall.

"My God! Since when are they early?" I asked.

"This is a first," said Shelly.

My knees weakened; my stomach quivered with anticipation. People started pushing towards the front of the room. I stood back and took a deep breath and held it. I pressed Owen against my chest, feeling the warmth of his reliable body against mine. The men poured in with their bags on their shoulders and their eyes scanning the room for their loved ones. Some of them had huge smiles across their faces despite the loss they'd experienced. Some came in averting their eyes, looking over everyone's heads. Others were unable to soak in the welcome; it was obvious they would not return home after all. Afghanistan is where they would stay.

I swayed my weight from one foot to another, searching the entrance for my handsome husband. I thought of a story I had heard about the young girl who ran after the bus when Steve left on his first tour. She ran after them, screaming, *"Noooooo! Noooooo!"* I thought she was crazy then. Weak. Now I could see myself doing the same.

And then he walked into the hall, tall and just as striking as I remembered. Even more so. *He's home.* I pushed my way against the crowd towards him. He hadn't seen us yet, but his eyes were still full of life. Oh, thank God. Maybe we'd be one of the lucky ones. I tried to squeeze through the husbands and wives and kids reuniting, hugging and kissing. I made it past the newlywed I had seen earlier. The young, pretty blond girl was weeping in her husband's arms. Owen was tightly wrapped inside mine. Then there he was, right in front of me, alive and well.

"Hey, there you are," he said. His bright smile made me feel like a schoolgirl again. My cheeks burned.

"Hey you, how was the journey home?" I asked as he hugged us both with his rucksack still on his shoulder.

"Long. Longest trip home yet. Let me take a look at my big boy," he said as he took Owen out of my arms.

"He just woke up."

"Right on time, eh, little man?"

My heart was pounding. I felt euphoric for the first time since bringing my son home from the hospital, over a year ago. My eyes watered as I watched them, now face to face.

"Daddy's home, Owen. Did you take care of your mom like I asked? I think you did a good job. Your mom looks very pretty," he said turning his gaze to me and smiling. He kissed me on the lips, and for once I believed—really believed—that all was well in the world.

"Hey man, good to be back, eh?" a soldier said as he patted Steve on the back. "I want you to meet Junior here."

"How old is he?" Steve asked.

"Four months old, man. He's gonna be a looker like his dad," he joked.

"Yeah, right. More like his mom. Your face is a rubber boot and this kid is cute. Congratulations. Really, I'm happy for you."

"Thanks, man. How old is your son?"

"Just turned thirteen months," I said.

"Jesus Murphy, I thought he was two years old! That kid's going to be a beast like his old man."

"You got that right—a crusher!"

"We should get together for some drinks one night, with the women, too."

"Sure, give me a call when you get settled in."

"All right brother, take care. I'm going to get myself a Tim Hortons triple-triple."

"Later." Steve turned to me. "Well, babe, just let me clear out of here and we'll go home. Sound good?"

"Sounds great."

Steve handed me Owen and headed to the receiving line, where a row of doctors and counsellors were checking in the troops. We followed. It was the last step before letting the soldiers go home. The last official piece of business.

"Welcome home, Sergeant Daniel," said a portly medic. "How you feeling?"

"Great," Steve answered.

"Good to hear. You must be tired?"

"A little, but it's good to be home."

"Must be."

"You ever been on tour, Corporal?" Steve asked.

"Not yet, Sergeant. Hope to be on Roto 3."

"Good."

"According to the paperwork, you had a mole removed while you were overseas, Sergeant. Any problems since then?"

"None."

"Very good. Well, that's all for tonight. You're cleared here. You just need to talk with the doctor next."

"Right."

"Welcome home, Sergeant," the doctor said as he shook Steve's hand.

"Thank you, sir."

"It must feel good to be back on Canadian soil after that tour."

"Sir, yes sir."

"Well, soldier, you know the drill. This isn't your first deployment."

"No sir."

"Any problems sleeping while you were in Afghanistan?"

"None."

Check.

"Any anxiety or stress that is out of the norm, Sergeant?"

"None, sir."

Check.

"We lost some good men, great soldiers during this rotation. Anything you need to talk about?"

"No sir. I'm fine. Can I go home now?"

"Yes, Sergeant Daniel, you're cleared. You need to report back day after tomorrow at 0900 hours."

"Okay, thank you, sir."

"Welcome home," said the doctor as he looked at us both. Steve walked out of the assembly line quickly, saying goodbye to the men he'd spent the last six months with. "See ya around, guys. Don't go spending all your money in one day."

"Right," yelled out his buddy Jason. "The wife's already spent that money! Don't do anything I wouldn't do tonight." Laughs and whistles filled the room.

"Yeah, yeah. I'll see you guys around. I can't say I'll miss any of you."

"All set?" I asked.

"All done, babe. I'm officially off military clock."

"Good, let's go home."

We walked into the dark night with the wind howling.

"Yikes, it's cold out here," he said, putting his arm around me. "Looks like there's enough snow for snowmobiling this year. Maybe Daddy's gonna buy one after all, Owen," Steve said as he strapped our son in.

"Do you want me to do that?"

"No, I think I got this."

I sat in the driver's seat and buckled myself in. Steve sat on the passenger side and pushed the seat back, making room for his long legs.

"You must be so tired."

"I'm getting there. Been up almost forty-eight hours straight."

"You didn't sleep on the plane?"

"No, some of the guys kept us up all night."

"Well, you'll be able to get some rest now. That is, until Owen wakes up."

"So, what time does my little guy wake up these days?"

"Around six thirty. But he sleeps through the night now. Thank God. Ever since I stopped nursing."

"He's grown so much. I really can't believe how much he's changed. Do you think he knows who I am?"

"Of course he does. I showed him pictures of you every day. And I've been showing him the video you made before you left."

"Good. Thanks, Dan."

We both stared out the windshield. Small snowflakes hit the glass, instantly turning into water.

"Almost home."

"It will be nice to sleep in my own bed again."

"I need to get used to sharing it again."

"I can sleep on the couch if you'd be more comfortable."

We looked at each other and laughed.

"I'm sure I'll adjust," I said. I pulled into the driveway.

"Wow, I can't believe the snow you guys have had this winter."

"Tell me about it."

"I see you're getting the hang of the plow."

"The neighbours had to save my ass a couple of times after I got stuck."

"I'll have to check the winch tomorrow."

"It's fine."

He untied his boots and put them on the rubber mat. Molly jumped on him, whimpering with joy. The house seemed in good enough order. The fridge was still humming. He had tried to fix it before he left, but I told him that it hadn't lasted long. I always said I married handsome over handy. I brought Owen upstairs, changed his diaper, and put him to bed while Steve looked around the house.

He grabbed a glass from the cupboard and turned on the tap. Drinking water from the tap was something he hadn't done for a long time. He helped himself to the banana bread I had made him and headed upstairs. He checked in on Owen.

"My God, my son is so big. He's perfect," he said as he softly rubbed his head. Steve kissed him goodnight and turned to me, putting his hands on my shoulders.

"Are you sure you don't want me to sleep on the couch? I'm used to sleeping on a crappy mattress."

"Very funny. Just take a shower and wash off your cooties."

"Yes, ma'am."

I lay in bed, overwhelmed by immense gratitude for Steve's safe return home. Relief washed over me, but then, an uneasiness returned, too. There was so much to show Steve to make sure Owen would stay on his routine and I had only one day to explain it all. I had wanted to take Owen to daycare to let Steve rest but he refused. He didn't want someone else spending the day with his son after he had missed so many days already.

"What do you think? Do I look like a beast or what?" he said as he stood there flexing his muscles in a short towel. "Six months of iron, baby," he said as he slapped his bicep.

"You look good, babe. Actually, you just keep getting more and more good-looking. It's not fair."

"Well, you look beautiful, too, my love. More beautiful than I remembered."

"What does that mean, exactly? You thought of me for six months as an ugly duckling?"

"No! I just mean you're also beautiful. I missed your big moon face and your lips, and these too…" he said as he grabbed my breasts.

"Oh, so you think you already earned your way there, do you?"

"I think so. I've been a very good boy. Have you been a good girl?"

"Always."

"I love you, Dan. More than ever. I really do," Steve said as he looked into my eyes.

I loosened the yellow-ribbon stays and gave myself to him once more.

5 | D-Day

I sat in the back of a mid-sized car. There was a driver in the front, a corporal. He was young and had a Spanish accent. He was also polite and knew my husband well, which is why he had volunteered to drive me. I could tell he was nervous. His driving was jerky and he hit the brakes suddenly and often. In the back seat beside me was Marco, Steve's best friend. He was the first person I thought to call. I looked out the window, watching the cars zip by us, filled with camping gear for the long weekend—happy people who were going to happy places. Owen, eighteen months old, was still at the babysitter's, well past his dinner. I had never left him for more than a day and now I was leaving him for more days than I'd be able to remember and he didn't even have enough diapers. We were driving to Kingston, the biggest hospital closest to where the sky fell.

I stashed away my tarot cards while Steve served in Afghanistan. Some things you don't want to know ahead of time. Once he returned home, though, I pulled them out of the bedside drawer where my favourite books and journals were stockpiled.

"There she goes again with her voodoo stuff."

"It's not voodoo, they're Celtic wisdom cards."

"Nothing wise about those cards or the people who use 'em."

"Don't worry. I stopped poking pins in your doll years ago."

"Whatever, Dan. Seems like a big waste of time to me."

"Don't you have a bike part to polish?"

When I was twelve, my babysitter taught me how to read with a regular playing deck. Carolyn was in her early twenties and had long black hair and glasses. She told me she was psychic and that her mother was, too.

"You can use this to spy on your boyfriends," she said. "The black suit warns you of a dark-haired girl and the red suit warns you of a light-haired girl. Depending which way they face, you know who's looking at who. The cards never lie."

After the cards, we moved on to palms.

"Okay. The first thing you need to know is that your left hand is your past and your right is your future," she said, bringing my right palm up under her nose.

"Wow! You have a lot of worry lines for such a young'un. It'll get better, sweetie, I promise," she said, sweeping my bangs off my forehead.

"I know," I said, brushing them back in place with my fingers.

"Now, let's move on to how many kids you'll have."

Later, I used the palm reading skills, but only when I was feeling really good at a party. It had become my barometer for how drunk I was, the way some people smoke and then regret it in the morning.

I always thought Steve criticized me for practising the tarot because he, too, somehow sensed the looming day that would alter us. Or maybe it was the fanatical Christian authority he grew up with. His parents would never approve of such sinful cards. Even Crazy Eights could lead to the devil.

There was one persistent card that revealed itself over and over when I did my three-card draw. A blue man was painted on the front of this card. He held lightning in one hand that caused a tiny person to fall out of a bowl that had flipped over. The little man was falling upside down while the blue man held both hands up like he was trying to scare me. It was called *The Changer*, and it was defined like this:

> Complete and sudden change. Alteration of the world as one
> knows it. Shocking or traumatic incident. Old habits overthrown.
> Breakdown.Routine destroyed. Revelation. Clarifying or cleansing
> event. Humility.

I would often redraw a three-card spread with the blue man already sitting on the table. I tried to ignore him, but he kept coming back. I made myself believe good change was coming, like the posting to Trenton that we both wanted.

The honeymoon phase after Afghanistan quickly dissipated. Soon, Steve was back at work and I was back to reality. He was already training for his next mission, while I was counting the days until he would leave us again—until I would have to keep everything together all the time because there was only me. With Steve home, I felt I could let go a little and rest, but with the pressure I'd been shouldering, I started to crumble instead. Slowly at first, until I could no longer brace the weight of it all. The thick and towering wall I had built to help me cope through all the years was collapsing, and I couldn't contain the landslide of pain that came down with it. Afghanistan had been my final challenge before I became undone.

I could smell the booze on him while he sat by my side. Marco was already celebrating Canada Day. July 1st was like the Super Bowl for the military, and the pre-show had begun. His face was red from being in the sun all day and he was wearing his combats, the same ones Steve wore to work.

Marco was one of those guys who was always getting himself into trouble, like Dennis the Menace. He was forever goading the limits, letting his wild and curly hair grow well past the appropriate military length, getting in fights with troops and breaking all his toys, like his motorcycle and jeep. Loud and offensive, he knew how to push my buttons. The fact that I was a feminist made me a fun target. He would openly admit to this. A typical conversation between Marco and I went like this:

"Hey, Dan, did Steve tell you about the strippers we hung out with in Ottawa?"

"Shut up, Marco."

"Dan, these girls were ve-ry naughty."

"Seriously, how can you talk like that when you have a daughter?"

"Don't worry, she'll be getting her own pole on her sweet sixteen."

"God, you make me sick."

This exchange went on for years, until I learned to stop encouraging him. Despite his flaws, he was the kind of guy you could count on and Steve respected him for that. He was a loyal friend, but they were more like brothers.

"How you holding up?"

"I just hope I can keep it together when I see him."

"You will, Dan. Steve's the strongest bastard I know, but you're no weakling either," he said, poking my arm. "We'll know more soon."

He put his arm around me and I laid my head against his shoulder. I let the tears fall for the first time since getting the news.

Steve was home barely a month when the fatigue rolled in and grounded me like a miasma. I didn't cry this time, the way I did after we lost our first baby. There was a dullness, however, that would not dissipate, the way you can't taste your food when you're sick. Every afternoon, all I wanted to do was sleep, but I persisted. I continued teaching and mothering until I collapsed into bed at 10:00. I plummeted to sleep easily, but then I'd wake up after an hour to spend the rest of the night staring at our speckled ceiling and listening to Steve snore on his back. Later, that's when I started hearing him call out to me in distress, in my dreams.

Eventually, exhaustion took over and I became immobile, my body stuck in cement. I could no longer move from my bed in the morning. There were times when I thought about just peeing in the bed. Steve left long before I did every day, so I did my best to hide my mental and physical decline from him, but I knew I couldn't keep the charade going much longer. I just couldn't be sick again. I didn't want to be sick again. I had a baby now, and Steve was back from Afghanistan. I was supposed to be happy. Finally, I surrendered.

"You need to find me a supply," I said to the school secretary.

"When do you need it for?"

"Now. I need it right now! I haven't slept for weeks!"

She looked at me dumbstruck. I didn't stay to explain. I walked out and went straight to bed.

Three days was as much as Steve could tolerate.

"When are you going to get yourself sorted out? You can't stay on the couch all day," he said.

"After doing it all for nine months, I'm sure you can give me until the end of the week," I said. "Aren't you some kind of super-soldier after all?"

"Just call your doctor," he said as he picked up the diaper bag I had packed.

The doctor was adamant. "Danielle, you're depressed," he said.

"I can't be, I'm not even crying. I'm just exhausted."

"You don't need to cry to be depressed. I want you to take some time off."

"I can't. I have the grade six testing and these kids are already behind."

"Never mind the damn test, Danielle. The kids will survive."

I tried to get better: massage therapy, reflexology, Reiki, meditation, talk therapy, and medication too—again. Talk therapy was a bust; slim pickings in Pembroke. Reflexology didn't seem to work. Meditation was hopeless at the time, and massage was only as good as it lasted. The Reiki practitioner did tell me that my heart chakra was blocked: "Your heart is broken. You have so much pain in your body for such a young woman," she said.

The meds eventually lifted me out of the depression, but it took longer than the first time. I returned to teach a month later to a very disenchanted principal and more pressure than ever to get the students ready for their provincial tests.

After we got married, our goal was to get a posting to Trenton. This would give our family stability. Tours overseas would no longer be obligatory. It was the closest thing to a regular job we could reach while still keeping Steve challenged and fulfilled in the army. The Trenton base was known for its jump school, where copious opportunities for growth were possible. I just wanted to move there so we could be together every night. Missing most of Owen's first year had saddened Steve as well: I could see it in his eyes, in the way he walked towards his truck for work in the morning.

"It's all happening too fast. I don't want to miss another day with Owen," Steve said when he got home from work. "I need to get that posting to Trenton." He gave Owen a smooch.

"I know, nothing like a baby in the house to show you just how fast our lives are zooming by," I said, taking Owen and bouncing him on my lap, his chubby legs wobbling. "That would be incredible, Steve," I said, half-believing it.

"I'm going to see who I can talk to, to make this happen," he said. I squeezed Owen in my arms, kissed the top of his head.

Three lingering weeks later, the decision came through. They had invested too much in him at Base Petawawa, and they were not going to let their golden boy get away. Someone at the top always stopped the transfer.

"We're never getting out of here," I snapped after Steve came home with the latest rejection—the posting had gone to someone else.

"Maybe next year," he said, tossing his maroon beret on the table.

"Yeah, right. They own us. I'm so fed up." I plunked Owen in his playpen. For the first time, Steve agreed.

"I may have a plan that could keep me around for a while," he said.

"There's a position called the UEO (Unit Emplaning Officer) that could keep me home and out of the field."

"You would do that? I mean, are you sure?"

"I'm sure. At least for a while," he said, getting up to grab Owen from his playpen. He sat him on his lap—all three of us at the table.

He started his new job a couple of weeks later. Most of his peers were stunned that Steve Daniel was working a desk. He was now the Aircell sergeant, responsible for coordinating parachute operations between Petawawa and Trenton. He was also home every night to tuck Owen into bed. We were fast becoming a boring, normal family, and I loved it.

One night, the green bags came out of the basement again. He'd been *voluntold* to teach the basic parachutist course in Trenton.

"On the road again…" I said, while scrubbing the dishes in the sink.

"I was wondering when you'd start."

"Can you blame me?"

"Jesus, Dan, this is good for us! It's an opportunity to network. You want that posting to Trenton, right?"

"I don't want to be married and endlessly alone," I said, seizing the tea towel from over my shoulder and belting it on the counter. "Why can't you stay with the UEO job? It was finally good for once."

"I'm not discussing this. It's a done deal."

"This is no guarantee besides more time apart," I yelled as he walked away.

"I'm so sick of this shit," he said, rushing back towards me, pointing his finger towards my chest. "Why don't you move back to Sudbury and live with your mom?"

"Don't tempt me, Steve. I'm so done. This is *not* a life!"

"Well, Dan, that's your problem. I'm never leaving the army!"

"Nice! You know, marriage is supposed to be a compromise, and for the last seven years, I'm the *only one* who's been compromising."

"Living with you is no picnic, either. You're always depressed and you never want to have sex,' he said, exposing his teeth.

"Screw you."

"You know, life's not that bad. You should see how the other half lives. Spend a day in Afghanistan and that'll cure your depression."

"I don't know how else to tell you that I need things to change," I screamed, pulling on the sides of my pants, bunches of cotton in each fist.

"Well, maybe it's time we go our separate ways," he said, and walked out.

Two weeks later, on a Sunday afternoon, I listened as he peeled his truck out of the driveway, on his way to teach in Trenton.

I kept telling myself it was love that made me stay.

He came home on weekends. I was encouraged to make the most of our time together. I smiled when he strode through the door on Fridays and continued to busy myself late into the night after he disappeared on Sundays, with laundry, schoolwork, and Owen.

Even before the four-week parachutist course he taught wrapped up, Steve was tasked to take a course in Trenton—another stellar opportunity for the family. This one was called the MFPI for short (Military Freefall Parachute Instructor Course.) At least he was no longer in Afghanistan, his parents told me. I should count my blessings. I continued to keep all the balls in the air as I feverishly counted down to summer holidays.

Steve had been gone nine weeks. The MFPI course was winding down. Two more weeks to go.

I had gone to another end-of-the-year staff party by a lake and arrived home later than usual on a school night. I had just put Owen to bed when the phone rang.

"Hey, babe, how was the staff party?"

"It was actually all right for once. I'm glad it was outside."

"That's great."

"And you? Any jumps today?"

"I had the best day! Seriously!"

"Why so special?" I asked, sinking into the corner chair of the living room.

"I don't know. The sun. The open road. I took the longest ride of my life on my bike tonight. I just couldn't get enough."

"Well, aren't you just living it up out there? You must be tired now."

"Exhausted, actually. Five jumps today."

"What? That's insane! How can they make you jump so many times in one day?" I remember him telling me that one jump was the equivalent of an eight-hour workday. It was exceedingly taxing on the body and the adrenaline alone could wipe you out.

"They're just trying to maximize the air time, cut down on the days we need the planes."

"Geez, that sounds like way too much. Get some rest over there. I'll see you tomorrow night for the big weekend."

He called two minutes later. He never called back after we said good-bye.

That was my thing.

"I just wanted to hear your voice one more time," he said.

"Well, this is a nice surprise. I'll see you in my dreams, Sergeant," I said, closing my eyes.

"I love you, Dan. I'm glad you're feeling better. We'll find a way to make this work, babe, for the both of us. I want us to be together until we're old and wrinkled and rocking in our chairs on that wraparound porch you always wanted."

"I really hope for that, too," I said.

I was holding a large box when I heard my name over the school intercom.

"Madame Fraser, line one."

The kids had finished school the day before and I was hoping it was not an irritable parent, displeased with their child's report card.

It takes approximately forty-five seconds to walk from my class to the front office. That is how long I had before lightning hit the ground around me and the blue man showed himself, both hands in the air. I had no warnings that morning—no intuitions, no dreams the night before. Just a summer morning filled with an endless blue sky where hope and possibility gleamed.

"C'est l'armée," the secretary whispered.

I took the phone and said hello.

"Dan, it's Jack, Jack Parsons."

"What's wrong?"

"Steve had an accident. He's in the hospital in Belleville. He's being transferred to Kingston."

"What?" I said, pushing my hair off my face.

"He got hurt on a jump. Might have broken both legs and hips. We'll know more soon."

"Oh my God," I said, palm against my forehead. I leaned against the secretary's mammoth desk.

"I was on the jump zone when it happened. I won't leave his side until you get here. The doc will be calling you soon. Stay there and wait for the call. It's going to be okay. Steve's a beast."

I waited in a room by the office for almost an hour. I could not speak to anyone. I paced. I sat. I stood. I thought of his motorcycle and how much he loved it. I thought of how heartbroken he would be to lose a summer of riding after waiting so long to put his bike on the road. I waited alone. I was a pro.

"Danielle, le téléphone, c'est pour toi," the secretary said as she handed me the phone.

"Is this Mrs. Daniel?"

"Yes, I'm Steve's wife," I said, standing with my hand against my chest.

"My name is Dr. Lane. I'm the emergency physician here at Belleville General. Your husband had a parachuting accident this afternoon."

"Yes, I know," I said.

"I'm sorry to tell you this, but your husband is paralyzed."

"What?" I said gripping a handful of hair. "I was told his legs were broken."

"No. We were hoping they were, but his back is broken. He's paralyzed. Waist-down... Mrs. Daniel?"

"Yes."

"I'm afraid this is permanent. He will not walk again. I'm sorry."

I handed the phone back to the secretary. Night crashed down on me, but my eyes couldn't adjust to the darkness. I wanted to collapse, I wanted to scream, I wanted to run, but I couldn't do any of those things. My legs would not move. Not one step. The secretary, who was also a military wife, was speaking to the doctor in her broken English.

"I am la secrétaire at Danielle's work," she said, her large blue eyes full of tears. She cried, but I couldn't. She looked at me as she listened to the doctor. He told her the same thing. Day had turned into night and it was never going to change back.

I don't remember how I got home, how I packed a bag of belongings, or how I ended up in the mid-sized car with the corporal in the front and Marco in the back. I don't remember speaking to my sitter and telling her I had to leave for Kingston and that my mom and my in-laws would be driving four hours from Sudbury to pick up Owen. But I do remember another call I received at the school right after the doctor hung up.

It was the military. Steve's RSM, his regimental sergeant major. His big boss.

"Mrs. Daniel, this is RSM Peters. I'm really sorry to hear about Steve."

"Me too," I said.

"I just wanted to let you know that it wasn't an equipment malfunction that caused the accident."

"What is that supposed to mean?"

"Well—"

"Are you seriously telling me it was Steve's fault? I just found out my husband is paralyzed and you call to tell me the army is not responsible?"

"I'm sorry. I'm not used to making these calls. It's just ... I thought you should know."

The drive from Petawawa to Kingston is three hours and thirty-nine minutes. That was how long I had to rebuild my dilapidated wall and make it tall and strong. A fortress.

I walked into the emergency department with a sure and quick step, while Marco and the corporal took their places in the waiting room.

"I'm looking for Steve Daniel, please," I said.

The nurse pointed to the first room across the hall. I could feel everyone's eyes on my back as I walked. I pushed the heavy golden curtain aside and saw his half-naked body lying under a bright light. Jack waved at me as he walked out, still talking on his cellphone, speaking military.

"Steve, I'm here," I said. His six-foot-three body filled the entire stretcher, his dark, muscular frame in contrast to the white sheet that covered his lower half. He was lying perfectly still and looking up at the ceiling. I hurried over to him and held his hand.

"I'm here, babe, I'm sorry it took so long," I said.

"Dan, I'm paralyzed," he whispered as a tear rolled down the side of his cheek. His gaze stayed on the ceiling. "It's permanent."

"I know, baby, I know. The doctor in Belleville called me. We're going to get through this," I said and kissed his forehead, touched the top of his bald head.

The doctor walked in chewing on an apple.

"You must be Mrs. Daniel?"

"I am."

"I'm the surgical resident. Are you aware that your husband is a paraplegic?"

"Yes," I said.

"Good. We need to wait a few days for the swelling to go down before we can go in. Your husband shattered a vertebra in his back due to the fall. He's T-11 complete, which means there is no hope he'll walk again. That might sound harsh, but there's no sense in giving people false hope. We will be fusing bone from his hip to his spine and then inserting metal rods to help keep his back straight. Mrs. Daniel, do you have any questions?" he asked. He continued to chew on his apple.

"None at this time," I said, and watched him exit the room.

"Steve—"

"He's right, Dan. I'd rather know right away."

I grasped his hand.

"Where's Owen?" he asked.

"I called my mom and your parents, and they're all heading to Pembroke tonight. I should call the sitter to check on him. I'll be right back, okay?"

"I'm glad you're here," he said as he squeezed my hand.

"I'm not going anywhere, I promise," I said, wiping his wet cheeks with the back of my hand.

I pushed the curtain aside, feeling everyone watching. I trudged out of their sight, around the first corner, and leaned into the wall, sinking to the cold, tiled floor. I watched an older man on foot, holding his gown closed, dragging his slippered feet against the floor as he stared forward. I let my head fall into my hands and sobbed.

I cursed the gods, the army, the heartless doctors, the blue man—I cursed them all.

6 | NCO

"The non-commissioned officer is often referred to as 'the backbone' of the Armed Forces." — Jordan Chapman, 1st Inf. Div. PAO

I was the pillow-tucker, the ice-chip-runner, and the oh-your-urine-bag-is-full-checker. I was devastated.

Steve had been paralyzed for seven days and seven nights. I was counting the minutes between his doses of medication. His spine was still severed. He was suffering with chills, nausea, and vomiting, despite the morphine pump, the praying, and the Reiki being sent by my aunts and other Reiki masters across the globe. Steve didn't believe in Reiki to promote healing, but he was willing to try anything at this point. The Percocets were making him hallucinate, too.

"Dan, let Molly in," he mumbled.

"I did, Steve. I already did," I said as I watched his teeth chatter, his lips split from the desert inside him.

The nurse came in every few hours to check on him and moved his body so he didn't develop pressure sores. "It's your worst nightmare," she said to me as she flipped his body from his back to his right side, using the sheets to help shift him. Twice a day, they pulled the blankets off of his legs, poked him with needles, and asked him to move his toes as I watched in painful silence. The toes didn't move. He couldn't feel them. He was queasy from all of the medication, but, without it, the pain was intolerable. He couldn't eat. My purpose was to keep him hydrated and make sure the nurses were on time with his next dose of barely there pain relief.

Steve's surgery was scheduled for the next day. The swelling had taken longer than expected to subside. The surgeon told us he would be reconnecting Steve's spine using a piece of bone from Steve's hip, exactly as the surgical resident had said.

"But this is only to prevent his spine from curving," his surgeon said as he scribbled something in his chart. His words hung over me like a net. "It won't change anything," he added.

A parade of khaki moved through the ICU. I knew the nurses were making an exception—a uniform is a powerful thing. Dozens of troops came daily from Petawawa, Trenton, and Ottawa. It was a comfort at first, to know people cared. Many of them had to see it with their own eyes: the golden boy had fallen from his post. They brought homemade cookies, cards, and well-wishes from others who were on course, overseas, or unable to visit—all of them uneasy and unsure of what to say. Marco came back with Wallace, Steve's other best friend. They brought Steve a toy horse from the gift shop, the kind you ride on a stick when you're a child. Why the hell not, they said.

Two of the soldiers from Steve's jump course came to see him the afternoon before the surgery.

"I'm Davis and this here is Humphreys," the taller one with shaggy brown hair said as he shook my hand.

"We were with Steve, in Trenton," he said, as if apologizing to me.

"We still can't believe it," the other said. "It's Steve, you know."

"Yes."

"Um, we brought his motorcycle helmet and his jacket. Just thought he'd want these, you know."

He dropped them into my arms, the weight bearing down, keeping me from tipping over with grief.

"Oh, geez, I'm sorry, we didn't want to upset you," said Davis.

"Of course not." I held my stomach in tight and smiled. "Do you want to see him?"

"Yeah, okay. For a minute," he said, looking at Humphreys who was still focusing on the floor.

"Who let these guys in?" Steve asked with a glint in his eyes.

"Hey, man, we had to come," said Davis, going in for the handshake like they played on the same basketball team.

"The guys say hi. They're thinkin' about you, buddy."

"Thanks."

"You look like shit, pretty boy," Davis said, laughing.

"It's the food in this place, it's worse than our ration packs."

"You'll get back on your feet soon. You're fucking Superman," said Davis.

"Yeah, nothing can keep you down. Airborne!" Humphreys shouted with more emphasis than I thought he had in him.

Steve took in a deep breath and gazed at the foot of his bed.

"This is permanent, boys," he said. "My jumping days are over."

The stillness was suffocating. We could hear the breathing machine through the wall in the next room attached to another patient, the sound of it pumping air into an elderly patient's lungs.

"Well, we should get going," Davis said. "We gotta get ready for tonight's jumps."

"Yeah," Humphrey said.

"Steve, you need your rest," I said.

We never saw those guys again.

"Can I get you something?" I asked.

"No."

"You sure?"

"You don't need to stay here."

"Where am I gonna go?"

"I mean in this marriage," he said, his dark eyes fixed on mine. "It's not going to be easy taking care of a cripple."

"Easy is boring," I said.

"I'm serious, Dan. It might be better if you left. For both of us."

"Must be the drugs talking," I said as I rearranged his blankets, pulling them over his feet.

"This isn't funny."

"Steve, save your energy. I'm not going anywhere," I said, taking a seat by his bedside.

We looked at each other for a long while, our eyes filling with tears. He reached for my hand and brought it to his mouth and kissed it, then pressed it against his face.

Steve's mother, father, brother, and brother's girlfriend arrived the same day. His sister, a nurse living in the United States, had also reached the hospital, with her boyfriend, having driven all the way from North Carolina. My mom was caring for Owen in our temporary accommodations on the Kingston base, where they sent us after two nights at the Holiday Inn.

I was glad to see Steve's family, but it did not give me a sense of relief.

I had never felt completely accepted by them, and the truth is, maybe I had never fully accepted them, either. His parents' extreme religious beliefs created an unremitting blockade between us, a climbing wall with no end. I tried to be polite and respectful when Steve and I were first married, but it was getting more difficult to remain courteous and not sell out my own soul in the process. I had taken Owen to their Seventh-Day Adventist church while Steve was serving in Afghanistan, knowing how much it would mean to them to have their first grandchild meet their church friends, even though the thought of it alone splattered my skin with red blotches. I sat beside my in-laws and held Owen for more than an hour while the pastor stood on his pulpit disgracing everyone for wearing jewellery, including wedding bands. Afterwards, I smiled. I shook hands. I paraded my son like he was Jesus himself and made a vow to never go back there again.

"Thanks for being here," I said as I reached my arms out to hug them.

"Thank the Lord for getting us all here safe," my father-in-law said.

I spent the next day trying to convince somebody, anybody, from Steve's family to sit with him in his room. They went in, but they didn't stay long, except for his sister, who helped insert the IV into his arm after the nurses poked him umpteen times without any success. His younger brother was especially distraught over Steve's accident. He refused to get in a car and walked back and forth from the hospital everyday while he was there. He walked for hours in his grief. The rest of the family took up residence in the waiting room.

"It's just so hard," his mother said about going into Steve's room.

I sucked in the sides of my cheeks, biting down on them before I spoke. "I could really use a break. I haven't slept for a week and it would be nice to know that someone is with him right now."

"That's not my son in there," his dad said, pointing down the long corridor, his eyes bulging. "He's on drugs!"

"He broke his back. He's suffering! Of course he's on drugs," I yelled as I walked away, leaving them all in the sitting room with the TV blaring and magazines spread across their laps.

After seven long days of waiting for the swelling to reduce and praying for a miracle, Steve had his operation to fuse his T-11 vertebrae to his spine. I said goodbye and watched him being wheeled through a set of double doors. I waited for almost five hours, in and out of the waiting room, skirting Steve's family, and seeking support mostly from

Marco and Wallace. I made countless appeals to the gods. I was ready to sacrifice anything.

"The operation went as planned," the surgeon said when he finally pushed through the pea-green doors.

"Okay," I said. "What does that mean, exactly?"

"It means that his back should heal without issue."

"So, is it possible, could it still be possible—"

"It's not. Ms. Fraser, the only thing that could make your husband walk again is a time machine."

As the surgeon strolled toward the elevators, I hurled the *People* and *Us* magazines across the room. I paced up and down the green-carpeted floor as my heart imploded.

"Jesus Christ!" I yelled, raking both hands through my hair. "What did we ever do to deserve this hell?"

Steve's parents stood there, frozen, and just watched me. I dropped down onto the floor and started to cry, pressing my knees against my chest and rocking myself. Then they walked away, mumbling to each other, as I continued to empty my pain into the air. My mother would have held me—she would have squeezed me until all of my tears were drained from my body. But she was taking care of Owen back at the PMQ.

Once Steve was out of recovery and back in his room, I sat by his side, applying cold compresses to his forehead. His parents came in later. The room felt crowded.

"I'm going to get some coffee," I said. I arrived fifteen minutes later and they had already left for the night.

"Dan, my parents told me what happened in the waiting room."

"What do you mean?"

"They said you had a breakdown and you were swearing and using God's name in vain and—"

"Are you freaking kidding me right now? You just had surgery and—"

"Dan, listen. I'm tired. I'm in pain. I don't need any more stress right now," he said, almost crying.

"I know."

"You have to apologize. You have to make it right."

"Apologize? For being heartbroken? No. I will *not* apologize for that. I can't even believe they told you. They are so twisted. How is this helping you?"

"Dan, this is not a request. Fix it. For me."

"Fine."

After an already unbearable day, I left the hospital, went to their hotel, and knocked on their door. They opened it, looking at me like I had kicked a dying dog.

"I'm sorry if I offended you earlier. I was hurting so much. It's been so hard."

"We forgive you," my father-in-law said. He pointed at my chest with his long and thick finger. "But don't you ever talk like that again."

I began to weep and lunged forward to hug him—much to my surprise. He backed away from me and patted my back awkwardly. "Just pray to Jesus. He will help you now," he said. My mother-in-law stood by his side, eyes glued to the floor and arms behind her back.

My mother, Owen, and I were staying in the emergency PMQ—the drab clapboard housing where women and their children were kept during domestic violence incidents on base in Kingston. The furniture was hard, with sharp edges, the couch had two cushions and wooden armrests. The floor was linoleum. It reminded me of the hospital where Steve was. There were two stark bedrooms. I shared one with Owen and my mom was in the other. We bought groceries, mostly for Owen. My mom and I still had no appetite. Outside, the garbage and recycling bins lined the rows of similar PMQs, the stench unbearable in the summer's heat. It was a temporary place, a forty-eight-hour kind of place without a working washer and dryer and a leaky air conditioner. It was not safe for a two-year-old, walking barefoot in the puddled water.

"There has to be something else available on base. I need to do Steve's laundry and Owen's too," I told assistant officer Jameson for the umpteenth time.

"Sorry, ma'am, but all other single PMQs are promised to officers whose families are visiting for summer vacation," he said.

"Look, I know we're not from this base, but I thought we were part of the same army. Please pass this on to your superior," I said one last time.

The definitive answer came back at 2:00 the following afternoon—there was nothing more they could do for us at CFB Kingston.

Well, I finally decided, if the commander of the base was not going to answer my phone calls, then I'd go to him. I marched up the stairs of the colonel's headquarters, determined.

"I'm looking for Colonel Wilson," I said, hauling myself military straight. His secretary looked at me, startled.

"I'm sorry, miss, but Colonel Wilson has left for the day."

"Where can I find him?"

"I'm unable to give you that information."

"Well, this can't wait till Monday. I'm from Petawawa and—"

"You're the one with the husband in that parachuting accident?" Her voice softened.

"Yes."

"You may be able to find him at the officers' mess," she said, then pursed her lips as if to suck back the words she had let out in a moment of weakness. "Hurry on, then."

I stepped through the double doors of the officers' mess flanked with large flags. Black and white photos of uniformed men plastered the walls. I wasn't sure what I was going to say, but I couldn't speak through one more middle-man. I pushed through another set of doors and heard laughter ahead. After turning the corner, four young soldiers dressed in uniform halted and watched me barrel down the hall. They looked confused and amused.

"Can you tell me where to find Colonel Wilson?"

"Oh yeah, he's in the mess," said one of the officers.

"Through here?" I nodded, my heart pounding through my summer cotton blouse.

"Yep."

The room was dimly lit despite the shining bright sun outside. The walls were panelled with dark wood and the bar displayed a broad overhead of shiny glasses. Uniformed men gathered at tall tables, standing with drinks in hand. Everyone seemed to notice me; there were no other women in the room. Their eyes followed me, as if they would lose me if they looked away.

"Where can I find Colonel Wilson?" I asked the first group of soldiers I came to. One of the men smiled slightly, showing his stained teeth. He pointed to the far table. I made my way towards the colonel. He didn't notice me, even though the other four men with puffy chests displaying multi-coloured stripes stopped and watched me approach their table. He finished his sentence before he turned around and saw me. His eyes widened as he swallowed the last of his drink and set it on the table.

"Colonel Wilson, my name is Danielle Fraser and my husband is Steve Daniel—the soldier who is lying paralyzed at Kingston General. Could I have a word with you please, sir?"

He tried to smile and exchanged a glance with the man next to him.

"Let's talk over here." We walked several tables away from the others. He cleared his throat. "What can I do for you?" he said, joining his hands together on the table.

"I know you don't know my husband, but he is, was—*is* one of the best soldiers in this army. He won the General Vance Award just before his accident. You know: the one voted by his peers *and* superiors. He gave so much to this military and—"

"I know. I've heard about his reputation in the Forces—"

"Well, sir, it seems that once you're down and broken, the army abandons you."

"Mrs. Daniel, I can assure you that is not the case—"

"I know we're not from here, but aren't we part of the same Armed Forces, sir?"

"Well, of course. It's just—"

"We're not officers?"

"There just isn't any place to put you," he replied sharply, knowing already what I was getting at. "Those PMQs have been promised to other members."

"You should know I'm here with my two-year-old son. We have sacrificed enough for this army. All I'm asking for is a safe place for my son where I can also do laundry. You are welcome to visit us to see for yourself, sir."

"That won't be necessary. I can see you are very distraught over this. I will look into it."

"Thank you," I said, using all of my strength not to let this man see me cry.

"I'll have someone call you this evening, Mrs. Daniel. And we're sorry about your husband's accident. It's a loss for us all."

I had no faith in the colonel. I returned to the PMQ and helped my mother pack up my son's things. I thought it best for him to return home, no matter the impending changes in our residence. I just wanted him safe and away from the base.

"I'm sad to see you go, Mom, but I just don't want Owen here anymore. It's causing me more anxiety."

"C'est correcte, Danielle. I understand. I'll take good care of him."

"Thank you for everything, Mom," I said, the lump in my throat swelling.

"Ne t'inquiète pas, chérie. You have nothing to worry about where Owen is concerned, but I'm so sorry I can't also be here for you. You're alone here," she said tucking my hair behind my ear.

"I'll be fine, Mom," I said, trying to convince myself, too.

"I want you to eat and get some sleep. You need to stay healthy."

"I know, Mom. I'll try."

I hugged Owen, smelling his hair, and quickly handed him over to my mom. "Okay, just go. Please call me when you guys get in."

"I love you, sweetheart."

I watched the van turn off the base and onto the main road, wiping my tear-streaked face with both hands.

The call came an hour later from Jameson: he would take me to a new barracks. I watched through the window as the navy Corolla pulled up the sidewalk. Officer Jameson hurried to help me to load my things into the trunk.

"I guess Colonel Wilson came around," he said.

"Guess so."

He drove a few minutes past the concrete buildings, where troops were running in boots, cadets and reservists training for the summer.

"This is it. You'll be staying in the RSM suite," he said, like it was a hotel at Disney World.

Home sweet home.

"You're in room H-16. I can take you there?"

"No, that'll be fine. Thanks," I said, taking the key from his hand.

I grabbed my bags and made my way inside. Loud metal music echoed through the halls. I passed by some guy with his door open, sitting on the bed shining his boots, wearing only underwear and dog tags. Another man in a towel was headed back from the showers. The hallway was dark. I hurried along to find H-16 at the other end of the building, and then pushed myself in and locked the door behind me. It was a large space with a living room, a separate bedroom, and a bathroom. Luckily, I couldn't hear the music from where I was. Outside the window, a man and woman in civilian clothes rode by on bikes. I shut the curtains and took off my pants and bra and climbed into another bed that wasn't mine. Without unpacking a thing, I rested my head on the pillow and fell into an exhausted sleep.

It was Saturday. I knew this because that's what it said on the news. I called Jameson early that morning to have him pick me up to visit Steve first thing.

"I'm sorry, Ms. Fraser, but someone else will be there to pick you up today. I was told to take my summer leave."

"Again? I mean, this is the third assisting officer since I got here."

"I'm really sorry."

"Can he be here at nine please?"

"Yes, I'll let him know."

The Corolla pulled up in front of the barracks at 9:00. A young officer sprang out of the car and introduced himself: "Good morning, Ms. Fraser, my name is Parker."

"Hello."

"I want you to know that I have Jameson's phone and the number is the same."

"Would you mind if I sat in the front?"

"Not at all. So, we're heading to the hospital this morning?"

"Yes."

We didn't say another word. I was happy not to have to make small talk. He pulled up to the front of the hospital and dropped me off.

"I, uh, just wanted to tell you that I know about your husband. I mean, my roommate's older brother was in basic training with him and he said he was the real deal, like G.I. fucking Joe. Pardon my French. I just wanted to tell you that."

"Thank you, Parker, and thanks for the ride."

"Sure. Call me when you'd like to get back to the shacks."

I walked towards the hospital and suddenly stopped in front of the doors, seeing myself in the reflection of the windows. I looked tired and older. My shoulders were slumped, my hair needed to be cut. I wanted my bed, my house, my son, my husband—I wanted my life back. I wanted to spend the summer riding our bikes like civilians.

I wanted to find that time machine.

7 | R & R

When I was fifteen, I invited my friends over for a sleepover. The Hairspray Gang. We teased out our hair and wore our bangs like mini Walls of China, tall and impenetrable. My mom was away, housesitting with my two younger brothers, taking care of my cousins' horses while I kept an eye on my father.

I couldn't sleep. My stomach was queasy from all the Peach Schnappes we had drunk. My friends were all fast asleep. They always held their liquor better.

I tossed and turned, looking at the blue glow of the clock every few minutes. My track and field posters looked like small doors on the wall. I pictured myself opening them and jumping into parallel worlds where I was the same but everything else was different. Around two in the morning, as I listened to the sound of the crickets in the nearby woods, I heard voices outside my bedroom window. I left it open at night because it was always so hot upstairs. I elbowed up to the sill and peered down into the well-lit street. I saw them: my father kissing another woman right in front of our house. I watched as he groped this blonde, who was wearing a white jean jacket and matching white jeans. His hands on her ass.

Steve suffered for my father's sins. Charged and presumed guilty—no proof necessary. I married a man with an employer who assigned him a mandatory leave to Budapest, where he was encouraged to get wasted, let loose, and indulge. The Canadian Army consistently organized brief deployments called R & R (Rest & Recuperation), ninety-six-hour mini-vacations in the kinds of places where you can order a redhead, brunette, or blonde straight from your hotel room. This was part of the overseas deployment—a package deal.

To be fair, Steve was the kind of man other wives wanted their husbands to spend their R & R with. Daniel was decent. Daniel was loyal. Still, that didn't stop my accusations. It didn't help that locals and interpreters had voted him as the most handsome soldier on the Canadian bases in Bosnia, Croatia, and Afghanistan.

"So, how was your leave?" I asked, trying to mute my suspicions.

"Over and closer to coming home."

"Well, you'd better not come back with herpes," I blurted.

"Seriously? You know me better than that."

"How do I really know what goes on there? You guys all cover for each other. We're the stupid ones for trusting you."

"I'm not that guy and you know it."

"People change, Steve."

"Whatever, Dan. I gotta go."

Night after night I tortured myself with every possible ugly scenario, stories of betrayal and humiliation that leaked into the days.

"So who are you hanging out with these days?"

"Same guys, really. I go on patrol, work out, read—that's about it."

"You're not sneaking one of the interpreters into your tent, are you? Or how about a female soldier? I'm sure they get their pick of the litter."

"Dan, just forget it. Nobody can even get close to me because I'd never let them."

"Nobody's perfect, Steve. People make mistakes."

"I know these tours are hard, but this has got to stop."

I was still the little girl sitting in the back of our family station wagon with the maroon interior as my dad drove through town, a king-size Player's Light dangling from his mouth as he gawked at the women on the sidewalk or in other cars, craning his neck to get a better look, not even trying to hide it. My mom and I would both be in the car, a matched set, the two of us with our olive skin. She'd always look the other way while I drilled him with fiery eyes through the vinyl back of his seat. Inside, I begged her to say something. She never did.

Four years of courtship and six years of marriage, and still my jealousy burned. Steve was losing patience.

"Keep this up, Dan, and I'll give you a reason to doubt me," he'd say.

I'd clamp down into silence until the minutes ran out and the phone line disconnected us, our fifteen minutes up for the week. I'd sit there holding the phone in my lap, angry with myself for not being able to trust the man I loved. I knew he was telling the truth. He wasn't anything like my father.

But four tours and all the training exercises away from home—like the one that took him to Jamaica for "Jungle Warfare" during my spring break, and the ones to England for the Cambrian Patrol, and to Daytona Beach during the American spring break—each one stoked my fear of betrayal. Both of us grew exhausted by the accusations.

"Does the army purposely pick these dates and places to break up families? Leaving on Valentine's Day for Daytona Beach?"

"It just worked out that way."

"Right, some bitter and divorced RSM wanting everyone around him to be just as miserable as he is."

"Dan, the world doesn't revolve around you."

"That's for sure. And the military doesn't give a crap about keeping families together. I think they want you all to be single so you'll agree to go anywhere, anytime. No dependents, no problems."

I was a junky feeding my jealous habit, self-sabotaging my marriage to a faithful man. No matter what he did or didn't do, nothing could change the ghostly scene I had witnessed outside my bedroom window.

Even though we had struggled in the past and our marriage was by no means perfect, the Seven-Year Itch never hit us, but that didn't stop his nurse from falling in love with him as I stood by and watched, mere weeks after the parachuting accident that changed our lives.

At first, I was grateful for the attention he was getting in the hospital, relieved he was in good hands and receiving one-on-one care. After three weeks in the Kingston ICU, he was moved to Ottawa for rehab and a new routine was set. I was staying in a hotel off Bank Street, where many military uniforms also stayed, in a suite with a kitchenette. I drove to the rehabilitation centre almost every day for three months. Even so, I knew the difference between relative comfort and another night in hell would often depend on a night nurse, most often a woman.

This was our new life. Steve shared a room with three other men, all of them paras and quads. Each of their lives, changed in an instant: Brent, a twenty-something who had hit a deer with his truck, was now a quadriplegic. Jonny, a young teacher, husband, and father to a six-month-old girl, snapped his neck while playing soccer; he too was a quadriplegic. Another man who had suffered a stroke was struggling to regain his mobility. They were bonded not by serving together in the deserts of Afghanistan, but by learning to survive where wheelchairs are the only method of transportation. Quadriplegics who thought paras had it easy and paras who wished they were amputees, all of them wishing for one single do-over.

We were four weeks into rehab, and hoping for a maximum of twelve. All we wanted was for Steve to come back home so we could be a family again and start the "new normal" the medicos kept talking about. His team insisted we take it one day at a time.

"How was your night last night?" I asked as I entered Steve's room.

"Good, my night was good. Lizette was on shift, so no worries." That's how it went for a while. I continued to deal with the red tape with our home renovations—our bathroom on the main floor was getting a para overhaul: an accessible toilet, sink, and shower. I still had to organize getting a ramp installed and a lift mounted along our staircase so Steve could sleep in his own bed again—our bed. All the bedrooms were on the second floor of our two-storey house.

I tried to push away the guilt, the deep ache of missing my only child, but it just became one more thing that sat heavy on my chest as Steve continued his rehab, learning to do everything all over again.

One afternoon, as we sat outside the hospital, shaded by the few trees, Steve turned the conversation to his nurse.

"So, I have some gossip for you," he said.

"Really?" I asked, thinking it was about one of the guys in the room.

"Last night, Lizette told me that her dad committed suicide. She's responsible now for making decisions about his businesses and properties."

"Oh," I said through my teeth.

"She was crying when she told me. Said she wasn't feeling supported by her husband. She feels lost. Alone."

"Doesn't she have friends she can talk to? You have enough to worry about, like dealing with your own shit," I said, digging my sandals into the ground.

"Jesus, Dan, have a heart. Her dad just killed himself."

"Yeah, and her husband isn't there for her. What does she want, a replacement?"

"Holy shit. Why does it always have to go there with you?"

"It doesn't. This just feels so wrong."

"Well, don't worry about it. Sorry I told you."

When I wasn't with Steve at the hospital or alone in my hotel room, I wandered the streets of downtown Ottawa, the city where Steve and I fell in love. We dated for four years while I was going to the University of Ottawa. He spent three summers working at the Connaught Ranges, thirty minutes from downtown where I lived, for the Canadian Forces Small Arms shooting competition. While he trained all week on the ranges, I worked at Eaton's at the mall, and then we spent our weekends together after the mall closed. There was the market we zigzagged through on Sundays, shopping for strawberries, cucumbers, and tomatoes with our small baskets, arms linked. The bars we danced in, late into the night with our friends; we'd rush home after to my apartment, our hands all over each other, our clothes scattered on the floor. The coffee shops we frequented, eating breakfast together on Saturdays and Sundays, ordering the special: scrambled eggs for me and sunny-side-up for him. The canal we skated across, raced each other down, where we talked about our future, for hours, together. The many streets we walked hand in hand, always touching, inebriated with young love, soaking up every minute we had together until Monday arrived again, until we went back to our individual worlds.

I now ambled among strangers, an empty shell, the memories of our younger selves haunting every road I crossed. The hole in my heart was gaping, and it didn't help that I spent most of my time away from the hospital alone. I started talking to the homeless; it seemed like they were the only ones I could relate to. Everyone else seemed so busy, distracted, and unaware of the bottomless pain that existed in the world. Every day, I gave money to a young man who sat in front of Starbucks.

"Thanks," he said. "You're not from around here, are you?"

"No. But I used to live here, when I was going to school. Where you from?" I asked.

"Sault Ste. Marie. I came out here to live with my sis but she kicked me out when her loser boyfriend moved in."

"I'm sorry," I said. "Do you mind if I sit?"

I sat on the ground beside him. People hurried past us, eyes fixed ahead.

"No worries. I have a plan. I'm going to start a program next fall. I just need to get an address first."

"There's help out there. I mean, if you want it."

"Yeah, but everyone says I need an address before they can help me."

A transit bus pulled up and a crowd of people tried to get out as others waited impatiently to get in.

"I don't mean to get personal, but why are you walking the streets?"

"Well, my husband is in rehab and—"

"Oh, sorry. I was in rehab once."

"No, I mean rehabilitation. He broke his back. He's paralyzed."

"Shit. Like permanently?"

"Yes."

"That totally blows."

"It does." We looked onto Rideau Street as people rushed to get from one place to another. We sat there, with only our eyes moving, together.

In September, the grandmothers went back to work. I should have been going back to work too, but I'd quit my teaching job. Owen came to Ottawa to live with me in our hotel. Every day, I'd take him with me to visit Steve. Everyone at the centre thought it was the cutest thing, watching a two-year-old push his daddy down the hall in his wheelchair. His chubby legs and diapered pants leaning forward as he pushed with all his might, his dimpled hands flat against the back of the black chair. He'd puff out his cheeks, his face red with determination, as the nurses cheered him on. He adored climbing into the wheelchair and having his dad take him for rides along the hospital corridors. The wheelchair had become an extension of his father. An extra, not a loss. Steve was elated to see Owen and spend time with him. They'd never been together so much. They high-fived each other every chance they had. Being with Owen was the only time Steve ever truly smiled while he was in rehab.

For me, it was heartbreaking, but I didn't let Steve see it. I still hadn't begun to properly grieve, to process everything that had happened and how much our lives had changed. I was busy making phone calls, driving back and forth, pushing away the depression I had just overcome only a couple of months before. I was terrified it would return with a vengeance and had already asked the doctor to double my dose. "It won't make a difference," he had said. "There's no pill to help you through this, Danielle." But I could not fall. I could not crumble. I couldn't take that chance.

During lunch in the cafeteria, I'd sit with Steve and his roommates. Most of the other tables were filled with older patients recuperating from strokes. When we first arrived, it was summer and young faces quickly filled the rehab facility. Bike accidents and sports injuries kept the beds full. One of the regulars at our table was Matt, who became a quadriplegic because of a mountain bike accident. He could move his legs but not his arms. His girlfriend was a medical student at the hospital, destined to be a physician, but they didn't last. She said it was just too hard. He was grief-stricken. His breakup also created unease among the other married men.

Often, I helped his tablemates open their bottles of juice and tried not to help as they struggled to reach their mouths with their forks. Steve had the use of his upper body, which made it easier for him to eat. Sitting at that table, I knew we were still one of the lucky ones.

Steve had always worked out and he didn't want that to change now, but he was not allowed to use the pool, his doctor said, because there was no point.

"He's T-11 complete. He's not going to walk. There's no medical reason for him to use the facilities," he said, pulling on the sleeves of his mauve pressed shirt. Steve sat opposite him. I always made a point of being present when his medical team met to discuss his progress. They had said that it was better for the patient when the family was involved in their rehabilitation.

"What about his mental health?" I said. "Isn't that also part of the rehab program?"

"Well, yes, but water isn't a cure-all," he said. The physiotherapist and occupational therapist frowned at the floor. The hierarchy within the medical team was clear. I was the only one speaking out in support of Steve's desire to use the pool.

"Why do we even bother meeting if you never listen to our suggestions?"

Steve sat quietly in his wheelchair. The army had made him stop questioning authority a long time ago. He respected the chain of command.

"I see this all the time: people keep hoping for a miracle, but it won't change a thing," said the doctor, his legs crossed and lips pursed.

"What is so wrong with having hope? You don't have the right to take our hope away," I said my voice trembling. "You're a doctor, you're not God."

He scoffed, almost choking on his laugh while he rolled his eyes and signed the permission slip. I stood and grabbed it from his hands.

"We will walk through these doors someday," I said as I marched out following Steve.

"Prove me wrong," he said.

The pool never seemed available when Steve tried to book it. Instead, he worked out in the gym with the antiquated equipment on the basement floor. Rather than buoying his spirits, though, the workouts left him feeling like a second-class broken soldier.

Every day, we spent time outside. I sat on a bench on the hospital grounds while Steve sat in his wheelchair.

"Another beautiful day," I said, feeling the rays against my cheeks.

"Yup, another summer day when I'm stuck in this place."

"I know, babe, we'll get you home soon."

"Not soon enough. I can't even stand the smell of this hospital anymore. It's not rehab, it's more like prison."

"I hate it, too."

"You don't have to come every day. I understand if you want a break from this hellhole."

"No. If you're here, then I'm here."

"Are we ever going to feel normal again?"

"I hope so. That's what the professionals keep saying."

"Right."

"We should go back in. It's almost one and you need to get fitted for your new chair."

"I'll meet you in there," he said, looking up at the blue sky.

Once, in Kingston, after Steve was transferred from the ICU into a private room, I crawled into bed with him. Not under the blankets, but at least I was beside him. It had been almost three weeks of not feeling his body against mine, just my hand on his. His bottom half felt cold, as if half of his body had died—the way it felt when I put my hands on my grandfather's hands when he lay in his coffin when I was twelve years old. I stretched out by Steve's side and we watched Dave Chappelle on DVD. It hurt him to laugh, as his stitches pulled. I cried in between the laughs, feeling his chilled hips beside mine.

In Ottawa, though, the men lived four in a room. No way I could get into his bed or even get close to him. Instead, I sat in a plastic chair by his bedside as he transferred in and out of his wheelchair. For months, I only held his hand and kissed his cheek as others watched. I walked into room 1151 in the morning and left after dinner with a sense of loneliness and despair I couldn't even share with my husband. While I repeatedly drove away from the rehab centre and crawled into my bed at the hotel, while I ate for one and watched mindless TV, his nurse Lizette continued to share her pain with my husband during her night shifts.

While I was denied the right to care for Steve after the sun went down, another woman took advantage of her position. Lizette helped bathe him and care for him through the long, vulnerable nights. She helped wash his body and transfer from shower-bench to wheelchair. She comforted him and made sure he was not alone, bringing him more pain medicine to subdue his discomfort. She listened when I couldn't because visiting hours were over. They bonded in their mutual pain and suffering. I'm sure Steve told her things he wasn't yet able to share with me. And I already knew that she was telling him things that were not supposed to be shared in a proper patient-nurse relationship. I pictured her sitting by his side, laughing at his jokes, twirling her wavy, blond hair around her fingers, touching him and staying until he fell asleep. She was comfortable in the world of paralysis, an expert, while I was still a baby bird, terrified of the sudden changes, unable to cope, my heart still broken.

One day, when I walked out of the elevator and into the main lobby of the rehab floor, three people looked up from the desk as I walked by. Only two made eye contact with me. One woman could not bring herself to look my way, even after I said hello and used her name, Lizette. She continued to stare at her chart. I glared at her strawberry blond, shoulder-length hair, her blue eyes, and peaches and cream skin. She seemed sure of herself as a nurse. I wondered what she looked like under her purple uniform. I questioned if she was capable of flirting without the nurse get-up. She was pretty, but not beautiful. I tried to convince myself there was nothing special about her.

My stomach churned, making me catch my breath and hold it until I felt like I was drowning. Then my adrenaline kicked in and I surfaced, heart pumping as I stomped into room 1151 almost gasping.

"Steve, we need to talk."

"About what? Is Owen okay?"

"He's fine. Can we go somewhere to talk? It's important."

"I have physio in ten minutes. Can it wait?"

"Right after, then."

I watched him practise his transfers now without the wooden slab, a piece of soft and sanded wood he used when he first got to the rehab to help support his weight when moving from his bed to his wheelchair. I watched the way he picked up his legs from the floor to the cot, using both arms. How he threw a medicine ball back to his physiotherapist, strengthening his core. I sat there and waited, trying to be pleasant, his cheerleader on the sidelines. I held my tongue as we said goodbye to the physiotherapist and all of the people who greeted us as we made our way outside.

The sun was shining. Only 10:30 in the morning and already hot. We went to our usual spot. I sat on the edge of the bench. He pulled up beside me in his chair. Put on his brakes.

"So, what's going on?" Steve said. "Is it the army?"

"No. Still waiting to see when they can start the renos. It has to go through another ten hands before they stamp it. They're having a hard time getting a second quote."

"Good old army with their quotes. So what is it, then?"

"Do you remember how I said I had a bad feeling about Lizette? About how she was crossing the line by telling you all those things?"

"Seriously? This is what you want to talk about? Dan, have you noticed? I'm fucking paralyzed. I can't screw anybody, even if I wanted to," he said slapping his hands against his lap, making his knees knock together.

"I know. I'm sorry, but she's in love with you. I can tell. You have to believe me," I cried, tears of frustration streaming down my face.

"For fuck's sakes. Enough! I'm not going to do this."

"Steve, please. Listen to me. Do you know how hard it is to leave you every night and stay in that stupid hotel? Not only do I have to deal with the military, the house, Owen, and everything else, but now I have to worry about Nurse-fucking-Betty making the moves on my husband?"

"*Stop.*"

"I can only handle so much! I want her moved. I don't want her going into your room anymore or being your nurse. Giving you a bath. Washing your dick. Touching you."

"Okay. You're delusional. She's a good nurse. She actually cares," he said leaning forward and pinching the skin between his eyes, his index finger and thumb.

"Sure she does. I'm sure she's planning her next move as we speak."

"You need to figure out a way to deal with this yourself. I've got enough going on, don't you think? I'm not going to embarrass myself by asking her to be moved."

"Then I will."

"No, you won't! This is done. Don't ever bring this up again," he said, glowering before he took the brakes off his wheelchair and wheeled away, thrusting the hospital door open and leaving me outside.

I didn't say a thing. Not even when his roommates joked about Lizette having a crush on him. How she attended only to Steve at night and always lingered in their room. I continued to visit during the day and leave after dinner, when visiting hours were over. I kept telling myself that he had the harder road, that he was the one in the wheelchair, and that I had no choice but to shelve this too.

I watched her reading her files, getting ready for her night shifts as I walked through the lobby and waited for the elevator. My body prickled with a quiet, seething anger. I looked at her. I glared through her clipboard. I wanted her to know that I knew. That no matter what, I knew the truth. She'd sometimes glance up and then look away again, back to her charts. Her face and neck were flushed.

Nurse Lizette eventually contacted Steve through social media after he left rehab. She had divorced her first husband, married again, and was unsatisfied once more. Was Steve planning to visit Ottawa anytime soon? She had married a quadriplegic, someone who had been a patient at the rehab centre. Only then did Steve clue in there was something off with this girl.

"Holy shit, Dan, you were right. That girl is nuts," he said.

I dropped my gaze, sliding my hands into my back pockets.

"I'm sorry I didn't believe you," he said, putting his hands on my hips.

"But in my defence, you thought everyone wanted me back then."

I knew it all along. I always believe what I see through my window. I used to carry jealousy in my pocket the way some carry gum.

8 | Operation Release

After a sheaf of written tests and a hailstorm of questions about sleep, anxiety, and suicide, the doctor concluded that Steve was not suffering from post-traumatic stress syndrome. When it came to high levels of stress, it seemed he had impeccable coping mechanisms. A poster boy, even still.

"You two are remarkable. The way you're dealing with this," the doctor said as we sat at his mahogany desk.

"We don't have a choice, really," said Steve.

"Sure, you do. You always have a choice."

"Well, there's no point in feeling sorry for yourself," said Steve. "That doesn't do anybody any good."

"We have a two-year-old to think about," I added.

"Just keep doing what you're doing, then, I guess. There's no need to see me anymore." He snapped the cap on his pen.

"Sounds good," said Steve.

"But you know, things might get worse when you get home," the doctor said, pointing his pen at Steve. "It's usually a very difficult transition. Remember what we talked about."

"I'm aware of that," Steve said.

I nodded in agreement and reached for his hand. A poster couple.

Steve had been home almost a month. He had been released shortly after Thanksgiving, more than three months after his accident. His medical team gathered around him as he transferred from his wheelchair to his new silver Toyota Tacoma truck equipped with hand controls. His medical team worried that the hour and a half drive home might be too taxing on his body, and his dad was to follow him to make sure he was not alone on the road.

Steve had earned his new driver's licence while at the Ottawa Rehab—ten hours of simulator training onsite at the hospital, overseen by his occupational therapist. The license had cost a whopping $500. Everything to do with accessibility cost the earth, including his independence on the road. Hand controls were affixed to the steering wheel. A spinner knob made it easier for him to turn the wheel: he didn't yet have the core strength to hold onto the steering wheel at 10 and 2 for long periods of time. A lever on his steering wheel acted as the gas and brakes. He caught on quickly. His experience driving all kinds of military jeeps and trucks made is easy for him to adapt to another way of driving. He was determined to drive himself home, even though the trip from Ottawa to Pembroke was 150 kilometres long and the autumn weather had covered the roads with a sheet of ice. It didn't ease any nerves knowing that the stretch of road to Pembroke was already known as "the death highway," with the highest accident rate in the province.

I waited and watched the clock as I primped the sofa cushions and picked up the trail of toys left behind by Owen. The renovations were still underway and no matter how often I nagged our case manager, a civilian nurse working at the base hospital, the contractor was still not moving forward on schedule with our wheelchair accessible makeover. The ramp from the garage into the house had been installed just a couple of days before, but the stair lift to the second floor would take much longer, another month according to the contractor. Instead, a hospital bed equipped with metal bars had been set up in our dining room. We'd be under the same roof, at least, but we'd have to continue to sleep apart.

He arrived two hours later, pulling up into the driveway with his father close behind. I hurried outside, walking Owen down the ramp as he parked the truck inside the garage.

"Welcome home," I said, grinning as I opened the door of his truck.

"Daddy's home!" Owen yelled and reached up, giving him a high-five.

"How was the drive?"

"Long," Steve said. "Not used to driving anymore. I need some pain meds."

"Well, let's get you inside, then."

"That's a nice-looking truck," Steve's dad said, walking up behind us. "It looks like it handled well on the road."

"Yeah. It's a smooth ride for a truck. Much smoother than the old Dodge," Steve said.

"Grandpa!" Owen shrieked as he ran and hugged his legs.

I got Steve's chair from the back of the tailgate, assembled the wheels to the frame, and sat the cushion on the seat.

"Thanks, Dan."

"Owen, why don't you show Daddy the new bathroom?"

Owen got behind the wheelchair and helped push Steve up the ramp. Steve rolled in with Owen behind him and I followed along with my father-in-law. It had been almost four months since Steve had been home.

"Wow, did you make that sign, Owen?" Steve asked.

Owen nodded, a wide smile across his face. *Welcome home, Daddy, we missed you.*

"Thank you so much," Steve said, wiping his eyes.

"Well, I should get going now," his father said.

"Already? You can stay for dinner."

"No, I'll let you folks get settled in. Welcome home, son," he said, shaking Steve's hand.

"Thank you for following me in."

"No problem. Now, Mr. Owen Daniel, you be a good boy for your mom and dad," he said, patting Owen on the back.

"Thank you." I wondered if I should hug him goodbye.

"All right, we'll talk to you later," he said, moving away from me.

I closed the door behind me and turned to Steve. "You're home. You're finally home!" I said, barely believing it myself. I bent down and hugged his neck as he touched my arms.

In the hospital there'd been little room for anything that might trigger the past. It was all hospital gowns and medication, cards and books—nothing to remind us of how we'd been before. But the house was a minefield of memories that made us ache for how we used to be: family photos, Steve's gym shoes, the dog leash, Owen's stroller—even the cleaning supplies triggered a deep sense of sadness. I used to make fun of him, the way he would swagger around the house barefoot on Sunday mornings listening to Patsy Cline with the Windex in one hand, Fantastic in the other.

"Seriously, you're double-fisting it now?"

"What. You should be happy you have a husband who cleans. Most wives complain about lazy husbands."

"Well, yeah, but you take it to the extreme. I'm considering buying you a holster for those supplies, Mr. Clean!" I joked.

He ran after me, trying to spritz me with the Windex. But that was before. Steve could no longer run after me, he could no longer explore the yard with Owen, or tinker on his motorcycle in the garage. He was no longer an infantry soldier, which was the only thing he had ever wanted to be. Four months after the accident, the Daniel family finally began to grieve.

On the first night after he came home, I climbed into his single bed in our dining room. It had been so long since we'd been close. He spooned me awkwardly, shifting heavily onto his side, tucking the urine bag behind his knees. I listened to the sound of his urine swish back and forth as he manoeuvred it out of sight. I took his arms and wrapped them around me.

"They still fit," I said.

"Guess so," he said.

"Are you happy to be home?"

"Yes. And no."

"Meaning?" I asked, already knowing what he meant.

"It's harder, to be here, in a way."

"Are you going to be okay?" I asked, listening for the truth between his words.

"Eventually," he said.

We listened to the cold October wind outside the dining room window. The trees leaned; the branches danced; the leaves fell.

During the last month of rehab, Steve had been allowed to leave the hospital on weekends and stay with me at the hotel. It was to help prepare him for the realities of the outside world. A transition of sorts. But when he got to my hotel, he couldn't get into the bathroom. The hotel clerk had assured us the room was accessible, but his chair would not fit through the door. He had to use the hotel lobby bathroom. It was our introduction to a new world where accessibility was not a right but a privilege.

In the hotel room, Steve said he wanted us to have sex.

"Don't you think it's too soon? I don't want to hurt you."

"Dan, I need to try. You don't understand."

I watched him insert the catheter, the urine being sucked into the tube and out into a plastic white dish. I sat on the side of the bed and waited for him to hand me the dish that I emptied into the toilet.

"How should we do this?" I asked.

"You're going to have to get on top of me."

I took off my pants and straddled him, careful not to put any weight on him. But there was no response when I stroked him. This had never been an issue with us before, and after a few minutes, I couldn't help but feel like I was failing. Tears rose to my eyes. He put his hand over mine and showed me what felt best without saying a word, and slowly, things began to work.

I held my weight while trying to help him enter. This wasn't the most romantic time we'd ever had, that was for sure.

"Is it in?" he asked.

"Yes," I answered. "Don't you feel it?"

"Not really."

Tears fell from my eyes and onto his face as I rocked above him.

"Dan. Are you okay?"

"This isn't working. You can't feel it. It's so wrong," I cried.

"I'm sorry. I just needed to know," he said as tears flooded his eyes, too.

"It's just too soon, maybe."

I got off him and we both lay there, on top of the sheets. I burrowed my head into his neck and sobbed.

At only twenty-nine and thirty years old, we put our sexual intimacy on hold for a long time—the way some put away a favourite pair of jeans that don't fit them anymore, still hoping one day to be able to wear them again. We tried to find our way back to each other several times, but the accumulation of Steve's medical procedures, our mutual emotional pain, and the inability to communicate honestly for fear of hurting each other prevented us from moving forward. It took us several years to honour and repair this part of our relationship again.

"I love you, Steve," I said as we lay together in our dining room, my voice quivering.

"I know."

I let the heartache surface in the safety of our home while he held me. He sniffled, and soon we were both crying. It didn't take long for the deep-down sobs to come pouring out of both of us. Loss was everywhere and in everything. It was in the awkward way he held me, in the way I bent down and kissed him as if he were a child. It was in all that was not said because we weren't ready to say any of it. It was in the vacancy of his eyes, in the hole in my heart, and in the fact that he sat and I stood, in a world where accessible washrooms were not accessible at all. I desperately wanted things to go back to the way they were, and that was the one thing that for sure would never, ever happen.

In that moment of shared sorrow, I thought maybe we'd be okay because at least we were weeping together. I remembered that saying: A family that eats together stays together. Maybe the same could be true of grieving.

A couple of weeks after he returned home, I made an appointment with the base psychologist. The soonest we could get was a month later. Steve didn't want to go, but I told him we needed to go as a couple.

"Do it for me," I said. "It's important to me."

I was trying to be proactive—no way was I going to let us become a statistic. We drove up the usual highway and stopped at the lights where the tanks edged the entrance to Base Petawawa. I put my hand on Steve's lap as he drove, wanting to believe that he could feel it there. We passed the mess hall and the shacks and continued to the back of the base, farther than either of us had ever been on base. There weren't many cars or people around and we were relieved not to have to see any familiar faces on our way there.

It had snowed the night before and the parking lot was covered with a blanket of white. The ramp that led to the front door of the building was also covered in snow. After bringing Steve his chair, it took everything I had to push him up the ramp to the door. He leaned forward and tried to open it as I held us steady from behind, feeling as though the grey sky was trying to swallow us. When we finally managed to wrench the door open, a set of stairs faced us. I got us inside, put the brakes on the chair, and went upstairs to ask how on earth we were expected to climb stairs. Finally, a thin, older woman with large glasses followed me downstairs with a large set of keys on a silver ring. She flashed Steve a three-second smile. We waited as she tried every key on the ring. None of them opened the glass door to the elevator lift. She told us to wait while she went to get assistance. A man in uniform came back a few moments later.

"The elevator isn't working," he said, and walked away.

Steve curled in his lips. I bit down hard on the inside of my cheek. Without saying a word, Steve opened the door to leave. I pushed him back down the ramp and across the parking lot to the truck. He hauled himself inside while I collapsed his wheelchair, manhandled it into the back, and slammed the tailgate.

"I'll be right back," I told him through the window.

"Don't bother," he said.

"Give me five minutes," I said.

He rolled his eyes, put the heat on high, and closed the window. I darted back into the building and went looking for the psychologist who was supposed to see us, barging through her door.

"You won't be seeing us today," I said, voice shaking.

"What's the matter?" she asked, her blue eyes as big as saucers.

"What's the matter is that this goddamn army doesn't have any respect."

"What happened?" she asked. The look of concern on her face seemed genuine.

"The elevator isn't working. Do you know how hard it was for Steve to come to base for the *first* time since his accident and ... it's not even working!"

"I'm sorry. I didn't know."

"Everyone's sorry but nobody cares."

"What can I do?"

"Who's in charge here? Take me there."

After several minutes, I was taken to an office with a small uniformed man sitting behind a desk. I didn't knock.

I explained what was going on, then said, "Did you not think to test the elevator *before* he got here?"

"I'm sorry. I thought somebody did."

"Of course. Typical army. Somebody else is responsible."

"We'll get it fixed—"

"Too late. I'll never get him back here again. Thanks for nothing."

"We didn't know."

"Your superior will be hearing about this," I said, jabbing his desk with my index finger.

I charged back down the stairs, thrust the door open, and stepped out into more falling snow. We drove home in silence.

Christmas decorations littered the grocery store. The holly, jolly music only made me want to scream as I zipped through the aisles. It had been a particularly difficult day. Steve had already had two leaks in his catheter and it wasn't even noon. I was a little relieved to be out of the house alone, despite hating grocery shopping, and had become quite good at zooming in and out and keeping my head down. I avoided making eye contact with anyone; too many friends skipped the aisles altogether after spotting me, as if paralysis was contagious.

Turning from the soup section to the salad dressings and soya sauce, I ran into a teacher from the school where I had taught.

"Danielle," she said, waving and walking toward me. "I'm so happy to see you. My goodness, you poor girl, I've been thinking about you so much. How are you?"

"I'm okay."

"You don't have to pretend with me, sweetie."

"Well, it's been hard, but we're getting there."

"We've all been thinking about you at school. We couldn't believe it when we heard the news."

"I'm sure."

She moved in close and looked around before she whispered: "Don't you think it would have been easier if he had died? You know … that way, you could have a fresh start?"

"What?" I asked, appalled.

"I mean, sure it would have been hard at first, but after, at least you'd be able to marry again, you know, sweetie?"

"I have to go," I said, moving my cart towards her, suppressing with difficulty the urge to ram her full-on.

"All right, dear. I'm glad we ran into each other like this. Please know we're all praying for you at the church."

I didn't bother with the rest of the grocery list. I went straight to the self-checkout, my head down, lifting it only to look for the fastest way to the door.

Driving home, I started to think of all the people who had not called or visited or even checked in to see how we were. Only a few colleagues out of the three schools where I had taught had bothered to send a card. The list of extended family and friends outside of Petawawa who hadn't acknowledged Steve's accident was long. I started to tailgate the guy in front of me and whacked the steering wheel with both palms as I skidded through the stop sign. My closest friend, Alice, who had been posted to Trenton, had disappointed me the most. She should have been here. She could have been here.

My cellphone rang. I was worried it was Steve, needing help.

"Hello?"

"Dan, where are you?"

"I'm on my way back from grocery shopping. Everything okay?"

"Yeah, but General Hillier is coming to the house."

"What?"

"He's coming over."

"Right now?"

"Yes. They wanted me to go in to 3RCR today because he wanted to see me, but I told them I was really not up to leaving today, so he's coming here—right now."

"Oh my God! The house is a mess and Owen—"

"He's good. He just woke up from his nap."

"Change his diaper and—"

"Don't worry about it. Just get back as soon as you can."

I shut my phone and stepped on the accelerator, forgetting what had just happened at the store. I peeled into our gravel driveway, lugged the bags into the house, shoved the food in the cupboards, wiped the kitchen countertops and table, sprayed some Febreze, tidied up the toys, and put Molly in the backyard. There was no time to vacuum. Steve was still in the washroom when I saw the black cars surrounding our house.

A phalanx of eight men, all dressed in uniform, their chests awash in coloured ribbons, walked up to our front door. I opened it to a tall wall of green. "Hello, come in," I said, holding Owen on my hip while Steve rolled in behind me.

"Hello, Mrs. Daniel," they each said, passing me to shake Steve's hand.

General Hillier was the chief of the defence staff, the top soldier in the Canadian Armed Forces. He had visited Steve once in Kingston and a few times at the Ottawa Rehabilitation Centre. He remembered my name and Owen's, too. He had hugged me when he saw me—the way a father would hug a daughter. I liked him. I could tell he was real by the way he looked into my eyes when he spoke to me and squeezed my hand when he asked, "How are you holding up?" He made me feel like the whole family served the nation. In fact, he told me so. "It's not just the man lying in that bed who has sacrificed for this country. I know how much families give up, too." If only they could have all been like him. I was happy he was here, and I knew how much his visits mattered to Steve. They had talked about Afghanistan and books and future plans. The general had even offered him a position in Ottawa, if Steve thought it was something that would interest him. He wasn't sure, but he was grateful. Everyone else at Base Petawawa had started to forget about him. There was talk in the beginning about Steve working in some capacity in his unit, 3RCR, but there was never any follow-through. He was on medical category—still in the army but not back at work.

"Hello, Sergeant," said the general. "I hope you don't mind that we barge in like this, but I told you I would check in on you and here I am."

"No, sir. It's fine. I'm sorry I wasn't able to meet you at the base—"

"I understand, Steve," the general said in his East Coast accent. "This gives us a chance to see your home and your family. How are you, Danielle?" he asked, rubbing Owen's belly while I still held him against me so he wouldn't act like a regular two-year-old.

"We're happy to be together again."

"It looks that way. You have a beautiful home," he said as he walked through to the dining room.

"Oh, that bed is here for now," I said. "We're just waiting for the lift to be installed."

"I see. Shouldn't that have been done by now, before Steve arrived?"

"Well, yes. I—"

"I'll see to it that it gets done."

"Thank you so much, sir."

"Your son must be happy to have his father home?"

"Yes, he is. It's so good to be out of that hospital," I said.

"I'm sure. Well, we won't be staying long. I just wanted to check in on you. I heard about what happened with the elevator. It's been resolved."

"Oh! Thank you, sir," I said, surprised.

"I'm happy you're back home with your family, Steve. You take care now and let me know if you have any concerns," he said, shaking his hand firmly.

"Thank you for coming, sir," Steve said. He seemed almost happy.

They left as swiftly as they arrived. General Hillier patted Owen's back, and the men trooped out the door. The procession of black cars disappeared as if they had never been there.

"Well, that doesn't happen every day," I said.

"Nope. Sure doesn't."

"It just goes to show you weren't a regular soldier."

Steve was still looking out the window, into the woods, across the road.

"You okay?"

"Great, never better," he said.

"Steve, talk to me."

"Not now," he said as he rolled away, back into the bathroom.

A few weeks after that elevator debacle, we received a phone call from the psychologist, who asked us to come back to the building. The elevator had been serviced and had worked for a while but, since they had last tested it, it was down again. Did we mind using the freight elevator instead? It would be the only way to see the doctor before Christmas. Steve agreed, after much resistance. I knew he was doing it for me.

We parked at the back of the building, where Dr. Pearl was waiting for us. "I'm so sorry about this," she said. She held open the door as soon as we got to the top of the ramp. "You shouldn't have to use this elevator, but I really wanted to see you both before Christmas."

"It's not your fault," I said.

We piled into the dark freight elevator, large enough for a jeep, where a man in uniform put a key into the keyhole and we inched our way up to the second floor. No one said a word.

Steve and I went through to her office; there were stacks of paper everywhere.

"Sorry for the mess," she said. "I'm still getting used to all of this. I've never worked on a base before."

Great. This should be interesting, I thought. A civvie doctor. I looked at Steve. I could tell by the set of his jaw that he was even less thrilled than I was.

"Take a rock," she said, pointing to a bowl on her desk overflowing with stones of various shapes, sizes, and colours. "Both of you, take a rock. You can keep it." She smiled.

Steve raised his eyebrows and couldn't hide his dismay. I was hoping things would get better, and fast, for both our sakes.

"First of all, I just want to apologize for that fiasco that took place last time you were here. I felt horrible about it, but I'm delighted you've agreed to see me again."

"Good old army," Steve said.

"Yes, I'm starting to see just how broken the system is. Horrifying, actually. I was hired just a couple of months ago and I just can't believe how fractured the counselling services are on this base. And there is so much need."

"I'm sure," I said.

"Between you and me, I can't believe we still have a Canadian military to speak of. It's a miracle, really."

Steve and I looked at her, both hoping for a 180 reversal—STAT.

"Well, enough about that. How have you been, Steven, since returning home?"

"Okay."

"I'm sure it hasn't been easy with everything—and your son. Who's taking care of him right now?"

"He's at daycare."

"Good. It's good to keep him in a routine. First of all, though, you should be so proud of yourselves for getting this far."

"Yes, well, we have each other to lean on," I said.

"And let's keep it that way. Most couples don't stay together when something like this happens. Those are the facts."

I exhaled. "We've been through more together than the average thirty-year-old couple. The army life isn't easy and the truth isn't common knowledge."

"The social workers here are in the dark ages and they don't like somebody from the outside telling them so, that's for sure," she said.

"Oh," I said, looking at Steve and rolling my eyes.

"Did you choose a rock?" she asked Steve.

"I'm sorry?"

"A rock. Which one did you choose?"

"I didn't. I don't want a rock," he said.

"You'd be surprised by how much these little things help during the day. I keep one in my pocket and rub it when I'm having a difficult moment."

"That's nice," Steve said.

"Yes," she said as she leaned in. Both of us pulled back, pressing into our seats. "I've been carrying the same stone in my pocket since my father died fifteen years ago. He molested me when I was a child," she whispered.

"Uh … I'm sorry," I said, struggling to look concerned while inside I was screaming: Is there anybody out there who can help us? For the love of Joseph, Mary, and sweet baby Jesus! Please? Somebody!

The drive home was quiet. We were heading back without a plan or any strategies in place to safeguard our marriage—despite the healing stones we carried in our pockets. Steve's was black and smooth. Mine was jagged and white with fine blood-red stripes. He tossed his stone out the window before we pulled into the driveway, while my stone stabbed through my pocket, piercing into my skin.

9 | Civvies

Steve made the decision on his own to leave the military. We didn't have any formal family meetings to discuss our options, nor did he speak with any military personnel about moving on. He never returned to work after his accident, except for medical appointments and physiotherapy. Four months after he completed his rehabilitation, he started the paperwork to retire from the Canadian Armed Forces. For thirteen years, he had been a frontline soldier—an infantryman and paratrooper. Anything else seemed unworthy.

"I want a fresh start," he said when he sat me down to tell me. "I need to do something where I'm not Sergeant Daniel. I'll go back to school."

The thought of no longer being a dependent in the Canadian military seemed a blessing. It's what I'd always dreamed of, the freedom to move when and where we wanted. To book a holiday and make plans without being called up at the last minute. To no longer be told where to go and for how long, regardless of the danger. To no longer live in fear. A new place, where military uniforms were unseen and unknown: it all seemed too good to be true. Gone would be the days when I worried about losing him, the way I had ever since we'd met. It had been thirteen months since Steve's parachuting accident, and we were leaving military life for good. Goodbye soldier; hello, civvies. I was ecstatic.

Thinking it would make things easier, we decided to move back north to Sudbury, where both of us were born and raised and where our families still lived. This time, we chose to build, and now and then, we travelled north to make decisions about the new house, picking out brick, flooring, countertops. Coming back to Pembroke was always difficult. We couldn't wait for our new beginning to start. We were both counting down to another life, existing in between endings and beginnings, before and after, old and new. Our friends must have noticed. They were visiting less often. By the time we were ready to move, we could count our friends on one hand.

These were exciting times, but Steve wasn't himself. He barely had an appetite and was growing thin, his muscular frame shrinking before my eyes. His medication made him queasy and unfocused; he complained his mind was foggy. He was still in pain—if only paralysis meant free from pain! His spine was still attached by a thread and this thread was the cause of intense agony: neuropathic blasts would detonate through his legs, causing them to vibrate wildly against the floor as they slipped off the foot support of his wheelchair. He'd straighten like a board, forced to lie back and watch his legs thump against the laminate. Much of his time was absorbed by taking care of himself—washing, dressing, using the washroom. The rest he spent with Owen and Molly. He said little during these winter months, retreating into his Finnish roots. He used to tell me that if he'd never married, he would have lived in Nunavut by himself in a cabin in the woods, like a Farley Mowat character. I never doubted him.

Christmas came, and Owen helped to bring some joy into the season, but nothing was the same. It was as if there had been a death in the family, and we were still in mourning. I thought about getting Steve a puppy, a lap dog. I asked at the local gas station, where I saw an ad tacked up on the notice board, and on the afternoon of Christmas Eve, I walked in the door with a small gift bag, the furry black head of a puppy the size of a doll sticking out.

"Where did he come from?" Steve asked, smiling despite himself.

"I found him online at a kennel near Golden Lake. He wasn't cheap, but he's a purebred. A Shih Tzu."

"What do you think, Owen, should we keep him?"

"Yes, Daddy!" Owen screamed and stomped his feet with joy.

"Do you like him, babe?" I asked.

"What should we name him?"

"How about Rocky? He looks like a fighter." I smiled and put the little dog on his lap.

But by the time the new year began, Steve's affection for Rocky was already waning. The cute little dog only made things worse. I had hoped the two would bond and bring some peace and contentment into Steve's life. Instead, it was just one more thing to deal with. Another struggle.

Rocky would mess on the floor and Steve would chase after him in his wheelchair, lurching to grab him and throw him outside. But the dog was too fast for him and too stubborn. Even Molly resented the intrusion. Not long after, for all our sakes, we gave him to a loving family who had another Shih Tzu, where he could be happy.

Finally, after nine months of waiting for our new home to be built, we hired movers to pack up our belongings, and in less than a day they'd boxed up our lives and labelled it neatly.

The day we left our Cape Cod house on one and a half acres—the place where Owen took his first steps, where I measured his height in the downstairs bathroom, where hundreds of deep-rooted red pines stood sentinel—I could not help but feel gutted. So many hopes and dreams were embedded in this house. So many lives unlived. I wanted to take the treehouse with us—Owen and I had sat atop its red roof, day after day, when Steve was away. We brought snacks and books, and lay on our backs watching the branches sway. We listened to the wind with our eyes closed and counted the insects as they buzzed by. I sang him songs from my childhood in my French mother tongue and then made up songs as we passed the time—waiting, always waiting. But it had been reinforced and set up so well by Steve and his friend Marco that we had to leave the treehouse there, anchored to the ground, like so many other things—full of story, left behind. Driving away from our old house for the last time, I already missed the trees. I held my hand against my chest as I tried to count them all. They stood in all their magnificence, waving goodbye in the wind.

Our bungalow was wheelchair accessible, in a new subdivision, a French community close to where we both grew up. The hallways were wide and the bathrooms were constructed with a wheel-in shower. Steve was finally able to get around without scuffing the walls. Closets were two-tiered and we even had a glass elevator that sat underneath the floor in the laundry room, waiting to be called up with the press of a button, thanks to Veteran's Affairs. The world was still wheelchair unfriendly, but at least our home had fewer obstacles.

Moving to suburbia was like moving to the desert after living by the sea. Foreign. I was not prepared for this new world of carefully carved-up parcels of land, on each of them two cars, two kids, a two-car garage. After living in the boonies among the trees and birds, where the only time you saw your closest neighbour was when they drove by on their to way to pick up the mail, this world seemed unreal, like a bizarre show on The Comedy Network. In the army, we never once lived in a neighbourhood where you could smell what the neighbours were cooking. Now, we had moved into a court governed by unwritten rules. Fraternizing with your neighbours was a must. Lawn etiquette was a science. The car was king.

Owen quickly made new friends in the cul-de-sac, where almost every backyard flashed a trampoline and a pool. I finally understood what "keeping up with the Joneses" meant, where a new interlocking brick driveway and fresh landscaping raised eyebrows and was discussed around the supper table. As much as people wanted to blend in, they also wanted to stand out in these planned neighbourhoods.

I soon warped into this new sphere. I watched out my window as the huge transport truck made yet another delivery two doors down, wondering what they had bought this time from the Brick. Gone were the days when I worried about life and death, roadside bombs, or marking off days on a calendar. I was now consumed with how to decorate our new home: modern, eclectic or shabby chic? I agonized over the types of blinds I should buy. I called them window treatments. I was becoming one of them.

"What's with the yellow ribbon around your tree?" asked my neighbour, a miner. He often lined up his trucks, cars, four-wheelers, and motorcycles in front of his house like Tonka trucks.

"Oh! You don't know?" I asked.

"Well, I know it's not for drinking and driving, 'cause those are red," he said, scratching his beard.

"The yellow ribbons are to support the troops—the Canadian military—the ones in Afghanistan right now."

"Ah. I never saw the yellow ones before."

I bit down on my tongue, grinned, and went back inside, kicking my shoes so hard they ricocheted off the wall. I was no longer an army wife; nor did I want to be. But, because of how intimately I had experienced that life and how fiercely I defended what Steve had given, I was not a civilian, either. I felt trapped between worlds, as if I didn't belong anywhere.

These culture gaps surfaced time and time again, no matter where I went: Pampered Chef parties, baby showers, Tim Hortons, neighbourhood barbecues; nobody was concerned about what was going on outside the suburbs. *Where are you guys going for spring break? You should see the boat my husband wants to buy. I think we're going to build another house, we've already outgrown this one.* When we lost soldiers overseas, it was never mentioned with the day-to-day weather or lawn troubleshooting conversations. It was always left unsaid. Business as usual. Commute in. Work. Commute out. Cut the lawn. Water the lawn. Wash the car. Bring Jimmy and Debbie to soccer. Walk the dog. Repeat.

Steve, on the other hand, had a live-and-let-live attitude with the neighbours, and he grew irritated with my fuming. "How can you stomach their ignorance?" I asked.

"Easy: I choose to see they're a product of their environment," he said. "This is a mining town. It's not personal."

"Not good enough," I said.

"They're not exposed to it."

"Well, I can fix that. It isn't right. This is still Canada," I grumbled.

"Dan, you should concentrate on moving on. Maybe living with our heads in the sand for a while isn't such a bad thing," he said.

"You know I can't live in the dark. I'm not made that way. I didn't think you were, either."

"Don't you think I know about reality? I live it every day in this fucking chair! I'm *aware*. I just choose to make the most of it."

"I'll never turn my back on the real world."

"We can't force the military down their throats. It doesn't work that way."

"Well, I can't tiptoe around their oblivious chitchat anymore. They have no clue what people lose while they wash their stupid cars every day. We're living in the freaking Twilight Zone!"

I grabbed my keys and headed for the door. "Why do you have to be a goddamn Buddha all the time?" I shouted, then slammed the door.

I drove around the new subdivision, past the new moms pushing their strollers and the dads in their shorts cutting their lawns in perfectly straight lines, then veered off the dirt road and onto the highway. I opened my window and let the cool afternoon breeze swirl through the car. I hung my arm out, letting the wind carry it up and down, up and down. I loved doing this. It felt childlike and rebellious all at once. I didn't know what else to do with the ball of anger bearing down on my chest. Days had turned into months and still it wasn't dissipating. I was angry with myself for not embracing our new life. I wanted to be happy, to count every blessing, but I wasn't done accepting the losses, never mind letting them all go.

I couldn't drive far enough. It was so hard to pretend all day. I wasn't okay. I was far from it. I pressed the gas down as far as it could go. Maybe if I went fast enough, the car would drift into the air, like my arm—like the birds. Instead, I continued on the ground, wheels against the gravel, watching the birds glide up and away.

An hour later, I made my way back, my foot was no longer leaden on the accelerator as I drove the same road to bring me back to the subdivision, to the court, to the new wheelchair accessible home, with one freshly planted tree in the front yard. A maple. I opened the door to find Steve and Owen playing with the Thomas trains. I sat on the floor and willed myself into the world of Thomas and Percy. If only I could be a train.

I was now a full-time, stay-at-home mom. Owen was only three and we'd lost so much time together already. I wanted to stay home with him before he started school. I had read all of the parenting books. I knew how important one to five-years-old was.

Even so, I missed having an outside life with friends and colleagues to talk to, a life in which I was not just a mother or wife but also a person with even more to contribute. I also missed getting a paycheque. We had always kept our finances separate. Now, I had to ask Steve if I could borrow his bank card just to buy a litre of milk.

We were fortunate that Steve was one of those soldiers who was going to get a pension: we made the cut by just a couple of months. The timing of his accident put him under the grandfather clause, so he'd get a monthly cheque instead of a single lump sum payment, like all the other wounded soldiers after him. We knew that we were lucky. That timing was everything.

At first, I dropped the words everywhere I went. Paralyzed. Paralysis. Paraplegic. *Yes, that means from the waist down.* Maybe I was still trying to believe it myself. This gig was permanent. My grief was so thick and garish in the beginning, like a flashing neon sign that never quit. I couldn't carry it on my own. Every person I told became someone else to share the bottomless sorrow with. I told my new hairdresser, the tattoo artist, friends of friends when I met them. "My husband had an accident. He's paralyzed." I held my losses up and out because they couldn't all fit inside. I didn't know where to put the pain. They'd cover their mouths and lower their eyes with genuine compassion and empathy. *I'm so sorry. I can't imagine. It must be so hard.* But sometimes, too often, sharing my grief would open the door to topics like the military. To Afghanistan. *We don't belong there. I'm embarrassed to be part of this war. That is not the Canada I want to live in. Canadians are peacekeepers. Why do we even have a military?*

I stopped oozing my pain, sharing my words, trying to find comfort and compassion. I changed the way I greeted new people I met. I started stowing it all inside—my body crammed like an overstuffed suitcase, all of the losses zipped up and compartmentalized.

Day after day, I played with Owen and struggled to be present in his world. I brought him to swimming class, art lessons, and soccer. I wanted to make up for missing so many milestones as I waited outside Steve's room all those months. I forced myself to meet other moms, thinking it would be good for Owen, and for me, too.

"So, are you from here?" a mom asked at swimming lessons one day. She was holding her baby girl on her lap, blowing on her belly and making her burst with laughter in between asking me questions.

"I grew up here, but I've been gone almost fourteen years."

"Wow. What brought you back home? What does your husband do?"

How to answer her questions? He gets up in the morning. He's learning how to dress himself, drive the car again, manage pain, learn marketable skills, and find a new identity. He's learning how complicated it is to live in an inaccessible world. She caught me watching her baby girl bounce up and down on her lap—those brown curls, the little pink barrettes.

"Do you only have the one?"

The anguish from admitting that I'd never have another child tore through my chest all the way down into my stomach and then back up to my throat where the words sat, refusing to move out into the air. How could I explain so much loss while she spoke baby-talk to her bouncing daughter?

They'd told us during Steve's rehab that it was still possible for us to have a baby. We'd visited one of those fertility clinics with glossy flyers and were told that I still had lots of viable eggs and Steve's sperm was somewhat active. The doctor we spoke to had a wall of baby photos behind him, proof of his talent that glinted in the afternoon sun as he ran his tongue over his teeth, shining his wide smile.

"You two are great candidates for in vitro fertilization," he said. "You're both still young and in good health. What do you say, should we add plus one to your family?"

He took down all of our personal information and medical histories, shook our hands, and sent us home with the glossy brochures filled with happy families. It was still possible. Maybe.

But Veteran Affairs would not cover the procedure. Our inability to conceive was a direct result of an accident Steve had while at work, but even so, they said, "they had to draw the line somewhere." Besides, they insisted, there was no guarantee.

It didn't matter. Whether they paid or not, I could not bear another loss. I could not risk another baby not making it. No matter how good the doctor said our odds were, no matter how many photos of smiling faces plastered his wall, I knew my heart could not tolerate anything going wrong.

"I don't think I can do it, Steve. I'm sorry," I told him as we drove back home to Pembroke from the fertility clinic in Ottawa.

"It's okay. You're the one who has to endure all the hormones and the needles and the actual procedure—it's your call," he said, disappointment dribbling through his words. But was it not having the baby or not being able to show the world that he could still have a baby that disappointed him more? I wasn't sure then.

"I just can't. Not now."

Sitting on the edge of the pool, staring at the little girl's chubby legs and rounded knees, I knew I would never hold another baby of my own again. I swallowed hard and let the pain bleed deep into my bones. Deeper still.

Only the one? The woman's eyes were still on me, waiting. She couldn't know how exhausting it was to explain, to answer such a simple question.

"We got lucky," I said as lightly as I could manage. "The first one was perfect."

Making good on his idea to go back to school, Steve registered at the college, his first time doing post-secondary studies. His first choice was university, but the military insurance company would pay for only two years of college. He chose business. Not that he liked business, but nothing else in the college brochure roused his interest even one iota. Steve felt uneasy about going back to school—now thirty-one, and after four tours overseas, he was going to school with seventeen-and eighteen-year-olds, most of them still living with their parents.

Even though I was happy for Steve and that he seemed able to move on so quickly, I envied him and his new beginning. I had always loved school. From time to time, I'd thought of going back myself, losing myself in books, surrounding myself with people and academia—for the learning, yes, but also to busy my mind again with things that weren't my life. But there was no tuition for me, and I already had my education—not one, but two degrees.

This made being a stay-at-home mom all the harder. I no longer recognized myself. Steve was meeting people and filling his time with something new, something that wasn't the army. Every day, he removed another layer of his former life. Meanwhile, I staggered on with my former world stuck to me like a hundred-pound rucksack—unable to remove any of it as I did the dishes or changed the sheets.

I wasn't proud of myself, but I was mired in self-pity, trying not to hate all the husbands who walked, who took out the garbage, who strolled hand in hand with their wives after dinner with their leashed dogs in the newly built neighbourhood. I tried to live like it didn't matter. As if I was still lucky, not slowly unravelling. I tried to convince myself to enjoy the moment as I watched Owen play on the floor. I read *The Power of Now, The Seat of the Soul,* and *The Secret,* aka the Law of Attraction. He's not going to be three forever, I told myself. Even so, I couldn't stay in the present. My mind would wander into the past. I wanted it back—the life where my husband could stand tall and hold me close. The one where he wrapped his arms around me and kissed my mouth, face to face.

The life where I mattered, too.

Tears bathed my face as I watched my beautiful boy playing with his wooden tracks. He handed me his favourite train. Even at three he was a wise little boy. I wiped the tears quickly away and forced a smile.

"Where is Percy going now, Owen?"

One evening, Steve rolled in from the college around 5:00. I was getting supper ready and stacking the dishwasher as the potatoes roasted and the chicken baked.

"What's for dinner tonight, sweetcakes?"

"Whatever's in the oven."

"Why so grumpy?"

"Oh, I don't know. Maybe I'm just getting sick of playing Susie Homemaker."

"I thought we had agreed this would be the best thing for Owen and for you."

"We did. It's just getting old."

"Well, you're the one who wanted to stay home with him."

"Either way, I lose," I said, that bullet of anger rising again, ready to ricochet. "Must be nice to be you."

"Oh yeah, real nice," he said.

I almost skidded I back-tracked so fast. "I mean, being where you are. Rebuilding. Meeting new people. Learning. Growing. Changing. Getting out of suburbia hell. Not feeling guilty about not being a stay-at-home-dad. All I do all day is wipe his bum, play with trains, and talk to moms I have nothing in common with. I'm losing my freaking mind!"

"Well, make a change, then," Steve said, "'cause I'm sick of coming home to a miserable wife."

A month later, I started making jewellery. In Pembroke, before Owen was born, I'd pass the lonely months stringing beads into necklaces that I sold to the other teachers. I'd lay the necklaces and matching earrings on the staff room tables and by 3:00 they'd all be gone.

That's what I would do, I decided. Make jewellery and bring in some money—my own money. I hosted a few jewellery parties and even approached local stores to sell my work: twisted copper-wired pieces filled with amethyst gemstones, jade and rose quartz, turquoise and tiger's eye combinations, and the classic onyx and moonstone favourite. I named them Copper Picassos. I lost myself in these stones and beads as I collected them, sorted them, and strung them together. They kept my hands and mind busy while Steve read his chapters and wrote his essays late into the night. I thought he would have more time for me—for us—after he left the army, but school took almost all of his time now. He had a new mission and he'd excel, I had no doubt of that. He'd be top of his class. Meanwhile, even though he was home from the war, I was still missing him, still waiting, still counting the hours, still lonely. He was right beside me, not off on a desert somewhere, but it didn't matter. I still felt alone.

I decided to put Owen in daycare twice a week to prepare him for the French school he'd be going to the next year. I told myself it would be good for him to have other kids to play with, but I knew it was good for me, too. I needed to find an outside purpose again. I needed to make myself a priority.

I began to treat my beading hobby like a business. I called it Creative Balance and made invoices and business cards. I had notebooks filled with possible logos and taglines, purchase sheets and inventory lists. I felt like I was creating a new domain, my own little world.

Steve continued to challenge himself in school, even though he was not crazy about the material he was learning. He was not a business guy, but he worked extremely hard and excelled in his first year of college. He soon began to grow in confidence and friendships despite the age and maturity gap. He made the best of it, as he always did.

Owen enjoyed going to the daycare with kids his own age. He made a fuss when it was time to take him home. He didn't want to leave, which the teachers said was a good sign. He was adapting well, but as he screamed to stay, I couldn't help thinking that I wasn't even fun enough for my three-year-old anymore.

The following week, I visited a downtown boutique with my jewellery tucked inside a clear plastic bin the size of a shoebox.

"Hello, my name is Danielle and—"

"We're not interested."

"But you haven't even seen it," I said, and held out my Tupperware with the lid still on.

"Are you planning on selling these anywhere else downtown?"

"Just a few places."

"Well, we're not interested."

"Are you the owner?" I asked, my breath quickening.

"No, I'm the manager. Why don't you open up your own shop?" she said.

"Maybe I will," I said, the rude rejection stinging my already fragile heart. "Besides, everything you sell is made in China. There's nothing special here," I added before walking out the door.

I tossed the box of necklaces and matching earrings I'd made into the back seat and went to pick up Owen at the daycare before it got dark. And then I hurried home to make supper. Again.

10 | Free Fall

I should become a professional wrestler. My name would be Mad Justice. I would stitch MJ on my chest and tie a tomato-red satin cape around my neck. It would flap behind me as I bounced into the ring. I'd wear badass boots and have really big hair teased on all sides.

Instead, I was an incensed domestic, stacking plates on the counter, squeezing too much soap under the hot running water, clenching my teeth in silence as the sink foamed.

It was weeks since the latest incident, but I couldn't let it go. Anger was now something I was comfortable with, like slipping on my favourite pair of jeans. I wasn't sure if it was growing up with my dad that made me this way or everything else that came after, but whatever the cause, my rage was building.

We'd gone as a family to the local Remembrance Day ceremony, the first one since the accident. Steve wanted to take Owen. He said it was time. I told him we'd go together.

That morning, he rolled out of the bathroom wearing his green wool uniform. He still looked like a soldier. I counted the medals on his chest: one, two, three, four. One for every six months-plus we were apart. His jump wings sewn above them, wide open like a bird about to take flight. Golden. I watched him leaning over, putting on his boots in his wheelchair with the brakes on. Black laces gripped in hands calloused from wheeling himself around. He laced them tightly, like he had done all those times before, even though he'd never walk in those boots again. Then he sat up tall in his chair and positioned his maroon beret on his cleanly shaved head. I had married such a gorgeous man.

Owen wore his good pants, black, with a thick sweater under his winter jacket. I wore black pants as well, with my grey turtleneck and black wool coat. Funeral clothes. All three of us with poppies pinned like splotches of blood to our chests.

Since we would all be separated on November 11, we decided to go to the local ceremony the day before. There, at least, we could remember together. But the hardest day we would spend apart. Ontario does not recognize Remembrance Day as a statutory holiday, thanks to the Legion, which had voted against it. On November 11, it would be business as usual where we lived.

As we approached the community building, a parade of cadets was already sliding into formation. Legion people strapped with medals and banners paced with equal parts of purpose and pride. This was their day.

My eyes scanned the perimeter of the building, looking for the way inside.

"Do you think there's another way in?" I asked.

"There better be. I see stairs, and a lot of them," Steve said as he pulled into the parking lot. I felt my jaw clench, my teeth grinding front to back. For God's sake, not today. "Just relax, Dan," he said. "We'll figure it out."

He'd barely brought the car to a stop when I swung open the car door and jumped out of my seat. At the back of the car, I clutched his wheelchair frame, attaching both wheels and rolling it towards the driver's side. Slowly, he transferred into the chair, the spasms in his legs shaking his body like a vibrator. When his legs stopped shaking, he picked them up with his hands and positioned his feet on the support plate at the front of his chair, strapping his feet in with a bungee cord so they wouldn't fall off without him knowing. We'd learned this the hard way: his feet had flopped over while his arms propelled the chair forward, jamming his feet under the metal frame. Several times, he could have fallen flat on his face. And then there were the times that he did. He pulled down on his jacket and straightened his beret, squeezing it against his head into proper placement.

"Let's go," he said as he wheeled ahead towards the cadets, legionnaires, and other spectators who had started to arrive. Owen and I followed hand in hand.

They looked at us like we didn't belong—the only ones with veteran plates in the parking lot. Empty faces looking on with no welcome or salutations, as though Steve had not in fact been prompted and persuaded to attend the ceremony by a local man who belonged to the Airborne Association.

"Excuse me," I asked an older woman legionnaire. "Where is the wheelchair access to this building?"

She looked around before answering me. Her eyes skimmed past Steve, then Owen, then me. Then she scanned her surroundings from side to side. A man stepped forward and spoke before she could open her mouth.

"I'm sorry, but I don't think this building is wheelchair accessible, Miss. We'll send someone in to find out."

"What the hell," I murmured under my breath.

Steve shot me a glare. I knew he wanted me to be careful with my language in front of Owen. I spoke to Owen in French while we waited, telling him the world still had so much to learn and this was one of those teachable moments. Owen just shook his head and agreed with me. He knew I was angry. Steve waited patiently without saying a word.

"I just spoke with the custodian and, I'm sorry, there is no handicap access," a legionnaire said, looking directly at Steve.

"This is unbelievable! How can you host a Remembrance ceremony in a building without wheelchair accessibility?"

"I'm sorry, we didn't know."

"You didn't know? You didn't know veterans might want to pay their respects to the fallen? What about other wheelchair users people who want to attend? Shame on you. Shame on all of you!" I yelled.

"Dan, that's enough. Let's go."

I took a step forward. "You have no idea how hard it was for my family to come here today," I said as I jabbed my index finger into my chest. "This was the first time since my husband's accident that we have been able to come and remember as a family, and we just got kicked in the face by the very people who are supposed to know better."

"We could carry him in," the man who had invited us hollered as he approached us. Had he known about this before? Was this his intention all along?

"Carry him in? He's a human being, a grown man!" I shouted.

"I just thought—"

"You thought wrong."

"Let's go, Dan. Now," Steve said. And I knew by his tone it was time.

"Mama, you were not nice to that man," Owen said in the car as we drove away.

"No, Owen, I wasn't. But sometimes you have to tell an asshole that he's an asshole," I said.

Steve eyeballed me, shook his head, and kept driving.

We were back home before 11:00. I couldn't wait to take off my funeral clothes. I kicked off my boots and threw my jacket on the chair.

"Aren't you going to say something?" I asked Steve.

"What do you want me to say?"

"Something. Anything! Aren't you pissed off?"

"Today was a really shitty day," he said.

"That's it?"

"Dan, I don't want to hear you bitch about this anymore. This day was—is—hard enough. I just want to forget about it." He rolled back into the bedroom to take off his uniform, boots, and poppy. He had long ago removed his beret. It had been sitting in his lap, an empty shell. I closed our bedroom door and led Owen to get changed, throwing his clothes into a heap beside his hamper. I knew it would bother Steve, but I left them on the floor anyway. I pulled Owen in close, his long legs dangling off the bed, and I held him against my chest, rocking him back and forth like when he was a baby. He let me hold him without saying a word.

December had arrived quickly, despite my ongoing resentment with November. I was unpacking the Christmas decorations; cradling the glass ornaments I had purchased our first Christmas as husband and wife—the one when Steve was serving in Bosnia.

"I don't think I can do it again," I said.

"Do what again?" he asked.

"Host Christmas. It's the last thing I want to do. I used to love Christmas."

"Dan, please. I don't have a large family like you. They're all I have."

"I know, but I keep feeling like I'm betraying myself. I can't stay quiet while I pass the mashed potatoes anymore."

"It's just one day. I want Owen to know his grandparents. I never had the chance to know mine."

Two years ago, we'd given Steve's parents the proper wood to build a ramp for their home, but still there was no ramp—and there never would be. No one ever spoke of this in the Daniel family. And I was forbidden to.

"Dear Heavenly Father, thank you for this meal we are about to eat.

We pray for mercy and forgiveness. We pray for those who are not here and those who are unable to eat a meal like this on Christmas Day. Bless the hands that made this meal, Father, and all those who are here tonight. We give thanks for the birth of your son on this joyous holy day. In God's name we pray. Amen."

I tried not to choke on my food as my father-in-law's words lingered over the table. I wanted them to know how much we struggled every day to get around in this world while they walked into their rampless home, said grace, and prayed for us to accept Jesus—according to them, only then would Steve's suffering end.

For almost a week after the holidays, I reminded Steve that I wouldn't be hosting his family for Christmas again, at least not for the next five years. He didn't fight me. But he did ask me to stop complaining about it. He was sick of hearing me go on.

I wanted him to call his mother. He said he would tell her next year. Why call her now? It would just make things awkward, he said. But what I really wanted was for him to be on my team. To demand respect for me. For us.

To tell them to build a ramp or else.

What I desperately needed was a change of scenery. Steve and I booked a trip to Las Vegas. We had never been there before and we couldn't wait to leave the snow behind. Owen was to stay with my mom for five nights. It would be our first holiday alone since he was born. We needed this time together.

The day before our trip, we went out to run errands. I watched as a large man pulled into the only vacant wheelchair parking spot. He leaped out of his vehicle and sprinted to the store entrance, while we circled the lot trying to find a wheelchair accessible spot. We were unsuccessful. The snow was wet and heavy. I pushed Steve through the thick slush.

"Can you believe that guy?"

"What *now*?"

"That guy who took the last wheelchair spot. I'm going to find him."

"Can't we just get some light bulbs without causing a scene?" he said.

"I'm sick of people like him. He needs to be called on it."

"You're right, Dan, some people are jerks. But you can't change them all."

"That's your opinion."

We bought our light bulbs, an extension cord, and windshield wiper fluid. I was holding the bags when I saw the man climb into his truck.

"Just let it go," Steve muttered, hoping for once that I could hold myself back.

"Someone's got to tell him," I answered, my heart pounding.

"You know you're parked in wheelchair parking?"

"I, uh, just ran into the store for, like, a minute," he said.

"Well, buddy, other people who *really* need it could use that spot. Hopefully karma doesn't bite your big, fat ass!"

He closed his door and started his truck. I watched him drive away and spin his tires onto the wet road. I heaved the chair back into the trunk after removing the slush from the wheels, and we rode home in silence.

"See, there are perks," Steve said to me as we were led first onto the plane. "Being a handicap has its benefits. We're like VIP."

I watched him transfer out of his wheelchair and into the airport aisle chair. Then I looked the flight attendant square in the face and said, "Be careful with that wheelchair. Last time, Air Canada broke it."

Steve stared at me. I turned away unapologetically. We waited for the next hundred and fifty people to pile into the plane. I was tired already and wished we could just teleport ourselves to the American desert. I looked over at Steve. He seemed calm and content.

"So, are you ready for Vegas?" Steve asked.

"Yes, I am. Bring it on," I said and closed my eyes, wishing all the people would disappear.

We were the first ones on, but the last ones off. I needed to pee. I watched as the flight attendants thanked every single person leaving the plane, smiling with their brightly painted lips but not with their eyes. Finally, two airport attendants came in with the aisle chair. Steve transferred into it, his legs trembling after not being able to stretch or move for seven hours. They pushed him out of the plane as I grabbed our carry-on luggage and followed. We eventually made our way towards the baggage carousel. Some guy rushing to get somewhere almost knocked Steve over. Mad Justice gripped his shirt before he connected with the chair and sent Steve to the floor.

"Hey, watch where you're going. Open your freaking eyes!" I said.

Steve was still wheeling forward. He didn't see what happened or hear the repulsion in my voice.

"I'm so sorry. I didn't see," the young guy said. He seemed sincere, but

I continued to glare at him until he walked away. We got our luggage and went to find a cab.

The taxi driver seemed confused at first. "You need a handicap taxi?" he asked.

"No, my chair breaks down, but can I sit in the front?" Steve said.

The driver nodded.

Steve transferred into the front seat while I hauled the luggage into the trunk. I went to get the chair as the driver reached for it.

"I got this," I told him. "Just hold the wheels." I detached them from the frame and watched to make sure the chair didn't get crushed as he closed the trunk.

"Our roles have reversed!" Steve shouted from the shower of our hotel suite later.

"What do you mean?" I asked, knowing full well what he was implying.

"Well, I used to be the hard-ass when I was in the army."

"Yup," I answered.

"Remember when I visited you in Ottawa with my buddies? We were such hotheads."

"Yeah, you Petawawa boys, always full of trouble."

He turned off the water. "Now *you* walk around wanting to throw a heavy all the time." He got out of the shower, transferring from shower bench to wheelchair. I didn't know how he managed to move his entire weight all day long.

"I guess so," I said. Now, he was kind and patient, the one who chose to see the best in everybody, the kind of guy who would end up with his own TV movie of the week. I was the one looking to throw down a body slam.

If only he could have known to skip his 160th parachute jump.

"Ready to hit the slots?" he asked, sliding the room key off the desk.

Vegas was a circus show for adults. Everything about it was grand. "This is a perfect world," he said beaming. "Everything here is so accessible." He felt welcomed there, like he belonged in society. It made me sad that the only place on earth that made him feel welcomed was the city with no heart and soul. We managed to get tickets to Cirque du Soleil's *O*. The show was sold out, but they usually reserved wheelchair seats. Perks. The performances were so beautiful I wanted to weep. But I breathed in deeply instead, worried that if I started, I would not be able to stop.

"In my next life, I'd like to be an acrobat," Steve whispered to me, wide-eyed. "That's pushing your body to the extreme."

I nodded, remembering how much he'd loved to free fall from ten thousand feet.

We rolled towards the elevator to get back to the main floor and watched twelve people pile into the elevator without even glancing our way.

"You have got to be kidding me," I said, the familiar rage rising within me.

"Just leave it! We'll get the next one," Steve said.

But Mad Justice could not let it go. "Hey, all of you with legs," I yelled. "Use the goddamn stairs!"

They looked at me, gobsmacked. Steve wheeled sharply away, distancing himself.

My cape flapped against my back and my teeth clenched. He wheeled back to me, and I stood behind him, like a shadow. And we waited.

11 | The Dependent

Two weeks after we were married, Steve left for Bosnia for six months, while I moved back to Sudbury to attend teacher's college. We wrote to each other every single day: *To my Handsome Husband; To my Beautiful Wife...* We were so giddy, so in love, and so full of hope about our future. Absence made our hearts grow fonder, and then some. He ended each letter by counting the sleeps until we saw each other again. I tucked his letters under my pillow and reached for them in the night.

When he came home for scheduled leave, he picked me up after school on a Friday and brought me to the airport. My bags were packed and I had no idea where we were going. I just knew we had to be back by Monday, for school.

We flew to Toronto, where we stayed in a modern-day castle with gorgeous walking trails surrounding the grounds. He had bought me the most beautiful dress with a black lace and beaded bodice, and a long cranberry velvet skirt (it was the '90s). It was stunning.

"I got help to pick it out," he said.

"It's perfect," I said.

We had dinner in a small, romantic Italian restaurant where we watched the candlelight glow against the window and the falling snow, covering the sidewalks with a blanket of white.

"Where are we going?" I asked for the hundredth time, touching his foot with mine while we shared our crème brûlée, licked our spoons.

"You'll find out soon enough," he said, his eyes twinkling. He reached for my hand. We ran out into the street, the snow still gently falling, catching on his eyelashes while he held me tight to keep me warm. We hailed a cab to The Princess of Wales Theatre, where we watched Les Misérables, the play about the book I had read in my French Lit class that I had loved so much. He remembered. We held hands for the entire show, including the intermission.

"I just want you to be happy," he whispered to me through my hair.

"I am," I said, smelling his sweet cologne, my heart bursting.

That night, I thought our love would last forever. Our marriage felt like a real-life fairy tale. I was his and he was mine, and our love story would live on happily ever after. The end.

And then, even this memory no longer felt like it was mine. It belonged to someone else—to two other people from a parallel universe where their love still burned, where they were still holding hands under the dancing snow.

I dragged my body out of bed after he left the room. It was just before 7:00 and it had been another restless night. The last few weeks had been the same: asleep by 9:00 and wide awake again from 3:00 to 6:00 in the morning. My mind was unable to relax and I flipped from side to side listening to Steve breathe on his back. By the time the sun finally rose, all I wanted to do was sink into the mattress. But Steve left long before Owen woke up for school. And so my tired arms would push the heap of blankets off my legs, and they'd fall heavily, one leg and then the other, off the bed onto the floor. Somehow I found the will to get up, to walk forward, and get my son ready for the day, preparing his breakfast, his lunch, getting him dressed for school and out the door.

I recognized the pattern. I knew this long series of sleepless nights flashed a bright red flag. I remembered the doctor asking me years before if I had trouble falling asleep or staying asleep.

"Staying asleep," I answered.

"A tell-tale sign of depression," he said.

It was happening again, the lethargy housing itself in my brain. I was too tired to fight it off before it burrowed into my body. I couldn't even rouse myself to tell anyone it was back. Why bother? I was already taking anti-depressants.

I slept through the afternoons, barely making it to lunchtime before the heaviness crushed me like a huge oak tree plummeting to the ground, axed at its thickest part. I gave into its weight and made my way slowly into the bedroom, closed the blinds, and crawled into bed, where breathing was almost bearable. These long naps became my shameful secret. All I wanted was to be alone in a dark room.

"You haven't been making any new stuff lately," Steve commented after several weeks of passing my worktable, beads strewn across its surface, untouched.

"Just been so tired. I didn't sleep well again last night."

"When are you going to snap out of this? You need to move on. Find some purpose again," he said.

"Roger that."

"You just can't sleep your life away. You eat like crap and you don't exercise. I'm getting sick of seeing it," he said crossing his arms, his muscles bulging.

"Well, we're not all born Superman."

"That's bullshit, Dan. Do you think it's easy for me to drag my carcass out of bed every day?"

"What can I say, Steve? I'm just not made of steel."

"The longer you wait, the harder it'll be for you to lose weight. Don't you even give a shit about yourself anymore?"

Owen was four and I still hadn't lost what I had gained when I was pregnant, never mind the weight my happy pills were adding to my body. This was part of his litany of questions when he used to call home from Afghanistan. To me, his comments about healthy eating and exercise were code for "it's about time you get your fat ass in gear." (He was the fittest guy in his unit.) I couldn't argue; I was too weary to even respond with any kind of dignity. I didn't have the energy to tell him that while he cemented the way for his new life, full of fresh opportunities, I was wilting from within. My world was a dark, lonely place. Any optimism I'd once felt was now barely a pale, flickering flame. The last thing I imagined doing was going to some gym to shake my thing.

As the weeks passed, we slowly shifted apart: two bodies living in the same house, slipping away from each other. The way a canoe can drift from shore if not tied properly. In the past, it would have shaken me into saying: Steve, we need to talk. But that was in the past.

One afternoon, he found me in a heap of darkness. It was 2:30 and he was home early from school. I was huddled in bed. He didn't say anything, just rolled in and rolled out. I could tell he was disgusted. He hated laziness. It was as if he had an allergy to it.

I forced myself to get out of bed, rake a comb through my unwashed hair, and pull on a pair of jeans from the laundry basket, struggling to pull up the zipper. I was far from the size six he had married—closer to a size twelve, my body swelling, distended with pain.

I wandered into the kitchen. "Where are you off to in such a hurry again?" I asked.

"I'm meeting a friend at the gym. Why don't you get a membership there?" he asked. His hair was neatly groomed and he wore a pressed shirt, sleeves rolled as he made himself lunch.

"I don't like working out in front of people."

"Well, you're not going lose weight hiding and sleeping the day away, either."

"Just go, okay. Go be Super-Steve and leave me alone." What I wanted to say was: *I'm stuck and I can't move forward. I'm sleeping because I'm depressed and alone and I need you, but needing you is a weakness you won't indulge.* Instead, I left him in the kitchen, eating his sandwich.

Steve became even more of a superhero. The Man Who Conquered Everything. He got involved in the local wheelchair basketball team. He was becoming something of a sensation at his college, literally a poster boy for their brochures, where he whipped through course after course with top marks. I watched as he picked up the pieces of his life, how he put them back together again. He was reinventing himself daily, as if his challenges were building blocks instead of barriers.

I wanted just a sliver of his strength, a single snippet of his DNA. Instead, my genes were encoded with the sadness chromosome. Both my father and grandfather suffered from depression, though they got the highs of the bipolar roller coaster as well as the lows. Steve had no idea what it felt like. He didn't want to know. He was the one in the wheelchair, yet he seemed fine. No matter what, that wheelchair meant that he would always win the prize for the hardest day, for the most improved, for getting his life back on track and fast.

"It's hard enough living like this," he said when he came home from the gym, striking the sides of his metal wheelchair, his wedding band ringing against the steel. "I don't need a depressed wife bringing me down every day. Something needs to change." I heard the *or else,* loud and clear. An old story.

His eyes held repugnance. I noticed the way he looked at my body, my stretch-marked stomach. It didn't help that he went to college with a bunch of eighteen-and nineteen-year-olds, their asses tight, their tits perky. I no longer undressed in front of him; I showered only after he was out of the house.

The more he pressed me about getting healthier, the more I defied him. I started eating chocolate during the day instead of having lunch. I was already skipping breakfast. I wanted anything that could be opened and brought to bed with me, and I ate it straight from the box or bag. I hid snacks and ate them while he was taking a shower at night, too embarrassed to eat anything in front of him that wasn't a fruit or a vegetable. I stashed chocolate rosebuds and macaroons in my purse and in the car—under the seat, not in the glove box where he might find them. Little hits of comfort always at my fingertips, numbing the pain and loneliness. Of course, I knew I was self-medicating.

We lived independently. His life. Her life. His school, his sports, his success. His spectacular metamorphosis. My dirty dishes, my unmade bed, my failure to move on. My dull evolution into domestic drudgery.

Steve wasn't married to the same person, but neither was I, and I just couldn't bring myself to tell him how devastated I still felt. I was afraid it might make him push me away more. But seeing elderly people holding hands was like being maimed by an arrow. I refused to go to weddings because it slammed me to watch people so close, nose against nose, and in each other's arms, while songs from before echoed within my grief-stricken shell. I ached because we couldn't make love the way we had before—I would try not to cry while I faced him, struggling to hide my sorrow so he would be spared. Having an orgasm alone made me lonelier than I could ever have imagined and I cried later in the darkness, unable to tell him that nothing was the same for me, either.

I felt as if I could no longer grieve these losses because he had stopped grieving; always a high achiever, he had moved on already. Or at least it seemed as though he had: he never lamented in front of me. If I brought it up, even in a roundabout way, he would say looking back was too hard; looking forward was the only choice. That I should do the same.

I was seething at him, at God, at the whole freaking Universe, that the first time he got hurt, he ended up *paraplegic*. That we had lost our first child and wouldn't have any more children after Owen. That he still expected me to love him the same, unconditionally, even though he was unable to love me with my broken heart, my shattered spirit, and my size twelve body. He did not love me the same. He could not love me the same. And, according to him, it was my fat ass that was bringing down the team. My healing apparently had a time limit on it. I should act like an ideal wife and put a smile on my face, too. Looking back was weak, a waste of time, unnecessary. Yes sir, Sergeant Daniel, sir. And, I was angry that he couldn't see my pain because he was the one sitting in the wheelchair.

I was the downer now, his weakest link instead of his life partner. Not the one who had stood by him through it all—the tours, the accident, the aftermath. I felt his disappointment in me every day. He didn't need to say the words.

Our two canoes had drifted into the void. Only a speck of red could be seen with the naked eye.

It was an early summer, and on this June morning, it was already scorching. Young artists from Israel, of all places, were making the rounds in our neighbourhood, selling original oil paintings. They did it every year in Canada. The woman who knocked on our door was pretty, with light brown hair and crystal blue eyes. She wore a cut-off shirt baring her slim midriff, and white shorts that flaunted her long legs. I watched Steve interact with her. He seemed overly friendly as he said a few phrases in her native language. Flirting. She blushed and pushed her bangs off her face, impressed that he had been to the Balkans. She wore thick eyeliner but didn't need it. She was naturally beautiful. He bought a piece of her art, a semi-abstract man and woman, facing each other, coloured blue. He flashed his smile, gave her the money, and closed the door.

"So, what do you think? Do you like it?" he asked as he held up the painting with a ridiculous grin on his face.

"It's horrible."

"What's your problem? I thought you liked art?"

"I do, but not what she's selling."

"God, you're negative."

"Sorry if I don't like watching you flirt with jailbait."

"She was in her twenties."

"Actually, Steve, I'm pissed that you're flirting right in front of me now. Who are you, anyways?"

"Well, maybe if you looked like her, I'd be more interested."

After several months of wretched days and desolate nights, I called Veterans Affairs. I was finally sick enough of myself to pick up the phone.

Getting therapy again was an uphill battle. Veterans Affairs had strict rules about who could see a therapist and for how long. As Steve's dependent, I was allowed approximately four sessions on my own. Four! I was allowed four more sessions if Steve accompanied me. We were also limited as to who we could see: the therapist had to be on the V.A.'s pre-approved list— which meant the wait times were ridiculous. Also, we could not see a social worker. It had to be a registered psychiatrist. The kind of therapist that can give you a pill and send you on your merry way after four sessions.

"Steve, please come with me. We need this," I pleaded.

"Dan, we've tried before. Those people are clueless. They have no idea what the military is like."

"I know the last one was bad. Okay, brutal. But we need to try again—for our marriage, for Owen."

Our first session was worse than bad. It was horrible. Yet we felt united in some way because we couldn't help but make eye contact with each other. We were so dismayed by his ignorance that we managed only three sessions because we could no longer stomach any more stories about his sixty-five-year-old wife and what they did to keep their connection strong. Hearing about them watching the local news together every night was not going to help us. We needed strategies. We needed an overhaul. The psychiatrist also made it clear that talking about our marriage before the accident was a waste of time and energy. "You need to focus on the present; never mind what happened before. Just let it go, Danielle," he scolded me, as if I were being an unreasonable, stubborn teen. But I needed to get it all out to be able to move on. Steve now had an ally because he, too, thought it was unnecessary to talk about before. Even so, the process left us both demoralized. Nobody was equipped to deal with military marriages. Nobody even tried.

"Don't ever ask me to go back to therapy."

"But there are others out there, and we need help."

"From what I can see, only people who need therapy become therapists. These people can't help us. I'm doing fine on my own."

"But we're not, Steve. We're not fine."

"I'm done with it, Dan. There's nothing more to say."

My therapy time was up; I had used up all my hours. I got on the phone again to convince our latest liaison person at Veterans Affairs that I was worthy of a few more sessions, even though by their standards, I should have been healed by now, or at least close enough to it to handle the rest on my own. But my heart was still broken. My grief was still there. Sorry to inconvenience the system, but I needed more time to work this out.

"We're just following protocol, Mrs. Daniel."

"It's Ms. Fraser, and screw protocol. Use us and abuse us, and if you break us, then you're done with us. That is the *army* way. The military has taken enough from us. They are not going to take my marriage, too! We are not healing together. We are barely together. For God's sake, can somebody fucking *help* us?" I said trembling at the kitchen table, phone gripped in both hands.

"I can understand your frustration."

"No, you can't. Ugh, I am so done begging for help. It shouldn't be this hard."

"I'll make some calls and see what I can do. I will call you tomorrow. I promise."

True to her word, she called me back by the end of the following day. Somehow, she managed to break the rules and get me eight more sessions with a counsellor from a list. It didn't have to be a psychiatrist or a psychologist this time, but it did have to be someone from their list. After two weeks of waiting for the paperwork and the insurance to be processed, I started seeing Beth. The one and only sane therapist I had met since the accident. Steve refused to go, despite my pleas that she was the real deal. I couldn't force him. His decision had been made.

I felt immediately at ease with Beth. She was motherly without being bossy. She had very kind green eyes and dark hair with wisps of grey. I could tell she had been through her share of heartbreak. Loss can smell loss. She was genuine and also cussed occasionally, which made me feel comfortable—I didn't have to worry about offending her. I felt like I could open up to her right away and I did. I had waited so long! And in that small office with the box of Kleenex in front of me, I purged it all. All of the junk I hadn't been able to share with anyone else: the indignation I felt towards Steve, the outrage I felt towards the military, my in-laws, the sense of abandonment, the disappointment towards my thinning list of friends.

"He doesn't acknowledge any of it before the accident. Like breaking his back gives him a free pass to wipe it all clean. Like paraplegia has anointed him a saint or something," I said, seizing one, two, four tissues from the Kleenex box.

"Tell me about it. About before the accident," said Beth, nestling into her chair.

"Well, I know I signed up for it, being a military wife and all, even though nobody tells you what it's *really* like before you get married—and hello, I was twenty-three years old when we married. He wasn't there for me, though, you know, even when he could have been—should have been," I said, tearing the tissues in my hands.

"When was that, Danielle? Give me a specific example."

"When we lost our first baby," I said. "He volunteered to go on course because he was sick of me crying. He just wanted me to get over it already."

"I can understand how lonely that would have been."

"Yeah, lonely is one word for it."

"Give me another, then."

"Abandoned."

"Is there another time you felt abandoned in your marriage?"

"Yes."

"Tell me about it."

I paused, staring at the painting that hung on the wall behind her, a water scene with two sailboats. My unspoken words hung in the air.

"It's just you and me here," she said.

"Well, after I had Owen," I said. "Less than two weeks after my emergency C-section, he left us alone, with no family nearby for help, to take a leadership course." Beth hadn't moved a muscle, both hands sitting in her lap. "Leadership?" I said. "So he could gain one more notch in his belt to move him up the ranks and add another precious bar to his sleeve. What kind of leader leaves his wife and newborn son behind when he doesn't have to?"

"How long was he gone for?"

"Three months. He came home one night in three months."

"That must have been very difficult."

"Yes, and after that came Afghanistan, all in the same year."

"It sounds to me like you were in survival mode during that year. How long after Afghanistan did Steve have his accident?"

"Four months later. I didn't even have a chance to really tell him how furious I was with him that he left me alone for nine months to take care of our baby. I was just relieved that he was still alive. That's what I was focused on at first, that we were still all together."

"I'm sure."

"I do admit that I fell into another depression in between his coming home and the accident," I said, lowering my eyes.

"Well, that doesn't surprise me. Your body was living in an acute state of stress for a whole year. You couldn't go on like that, without any support, and not have it affect you. Just hearing this information alone,

I can comprehend the reasons for your anger and sadness. You're only human."

"To be honest, I don't think our marriage would have withstood another tour overseas. I had reached my limit."

"Did Steve know this?"

"Oh, he knew. I was given my marching orders."

"What do you mean?"

"He told me he would choose the army over our marriage. That I would lose, so I shouldn't even bother asking. So I didn't. And then he went away again on that stupid parachuting course, and he broke his back. And, well, now we're here."

"You forgot the other part," said Beth.

"Which other part?"

"The part where you stood by his side for the last two years and helped him through his recovery. The part where you left your job and your life, to help his. The part where you loved him unconditionally."

"Yeah, there was that, too," I said snatching another tissue.

"Danielle, you have every right to be pissed off. To feel angry. I want you to know that you are not alone here."

One person in the whole world accepted my pain without asking me to shelve it or minimize it.

After several weeks of counselling with Beth, I began to thoughtfully examine our marriage before and after the accident. I realized that Steve would never have stopped trying to climb the ladder. Never.

It was in Beth's office that I learned how much I hated myself, how ugly I believed I was, and how much grief I had been carrying for years inside my bones. Beth helped me to connect my childhood to my shattered self-worth and my ongoing tolerance for receiving conditional love.

"Tell me more about your father."

"Oh boy."

"It's up to you, but I think it would help you see things more clearly with Steve. The patterns, I mean."

"Well, what can I say? I was terrified of him. He was a bad drunk. He still is, which is why I can't be around him. Christmas morning was happy and jolly, but by the time the sun went down, the Christmas tree was flung against the walls and so were all our gifts, because we were 'all a bunch of fucking spoiled brats.' He's abusive and a genuine bully. He remembers only what he wants to remember, and I can't be in a relationship with someone who doesn't admit the truth. I just wish he would respect my boundaries and stay away, like I ask."

"Okay. That's a lot of stuff," Beth said with a smirk.

"Are you sorry you asked?"

"Not at all. Let's go back. Tell me."

"I used to feel sorry for him. I know his childhood was a difficult one, so for years I gave him another chance and another, and a hundred others, until I had Owen. That's when I knew I couldn't tolerate it anymore. I had to protect Owen and myself."

"When were you most afraid of him?"

"After he got home from a night of drinking. He wouldn't let any of us sleep. He would blare his music and yell for my mom from the downstairs kitchen table. Most nights I would get up and beg him to be quiet and my mom would stay in her room, while my two younger brothers tried to sleep. I became his punching bag of sorts. He called me every name in the book. The c-word was his personal favourite."

"That sounds horrible."

"I don't know what bothered me more, knowing he was home and hearing him shout from the kitchen or lying awake in bed wondering when he would burst through that door. Sometimes he would bring his loser friends over. I was always on high alert. I'm still a light sleeper. He would be gone for days. Weeks even. My mom never talked about his absence; she was a good Catholic wife. We finally found out my father had left for good when my younger brother, while out with friends, saw him at a red light with a blonde." I took a deep breath. "I can't fix them. I used to think that was my job. Now, I just want to fix myself."

"Well, it's no wonder you struggle with self-esteem and trust issues, not to mention knowing what a healthy relationship should feel like. But you can work on this, Danielle. You don't have to be that little girl, waiting for her father to barge in, trying to protect her mother, or worrying about her husband cheating on her."

Steve noticed a change in me. After several months in therapy, I was now working towards opening a shop with my cousin, giving classes on beading and sewing. It was something I had wanted to do in Petawawa before Steve's accident, but I hadn't had a chance to make it happen.

"I just don't understand why you won't go back to teaching."

"Because I don't want to teach anymore. It suffocates me. I want to do something creative. I need a new beginning, too."

"Well, Dan, I'm taking business right now and I know for a fact that most businesses fail in the first year."

"Thanks for your stellar support, Steve. I can always count on you to give me a good dose of encouragement."

"Whatever. Just keep me out of it. You're on your own with this."

My days were becoming full again. I was slowly emerging out of my depression with continued talk-therapy and medication. I started to build a solid business plan with my cousin and realized that creating something new was feeding me.

Still, I begged Steve to get plugged into our marriage, to spend more time together, to care more. Instead, he focused on the outside world, on everything except his family. He met a woman through wheelchair basketball who invited him to try adaptive rowing. It wasn't long until he broke the Canadian indoor championship record. He had been rowing only for a few months and now he had a new challenge. Because of his success, he was invited to try out for the national rowing team to represent Canada at the 2008 Beijing Paralympics. He made the team. Steve created a binder with his sports psychologist, marked "Beijing 2008" on the cover. It sat on our kitchen counter. It might as well have been his orders for a new mission overseas to Afghanistan.

He was now preparing for the Games. His days were filled with school, training, and motivational speaking. Our family was still in second or third or fifth place, too far behind him for him to see us clearly, and I was beyond tired of living my life alone. It was hard enough to tolerate when he was overseas, calling from a satellite phone; now, he was in the next room, less than twenty steps away. It might as well have been oceans between us.

In the beginning, I prayed the accident would change things for the better. I would finally have him home. I wouldn't have to share him with the army anymore. I knew our marriage was in the danger zone after Afghanistan, and I thought his grounding would save us. Instead, he just substituted his obligation to the military with commitment to his sport. Transferred allegiance from the generals, lieutenants, and his comrades in the field to his coaches and teammates, all the people who wanted him to shine, once again.

After months of therapy, I finally accepted that my marriage was on its last legs. Screwing up my courage, I marched into his office for one last desperate appeal.

"Steve, do you have a minute?"

"Not really. Can it wait?"

"No, it can't."

"What is it? I have to send out this email."

"Steve, you know that I love you," I said, careful with my words. "I do. I still love you. But I just can't go on like this." My eyes filled with tears.

"This hasn't been fun for me, either."

"I know. It's just … I'm so tired of fighting and asking for things to change, and I … just can't do it anymore."

"So what are you saying?" he said, finally turning his body towards me.

"I'm saying that I need you to be the one to fight right now—for us. I have given you all I have. Everything. For years."

"Shouldn't it be a two-way street?" he said, pushing himself away from his desk.

"It's never been a two-way street," I shot back. "It's always been what you've wanted and what you've needed while I've waited for you. I'm done waiting."

"Nobody asked you to."

"Well, that's what a marriage is, Steve, and, for the last ten years, I'm the only one who has compromised in this marriage."

"I'm doing the best I can right now, with school and rowing and—I don't see how I can give anymore. Maybe I just can't give you what you need."

"Steve, I'm begging you. I'm in overdraft here. I have nothing left," I said, exposing my empty hands. "If you want to stay married, you need to try harder. You need to be all in."

He nodded his head. "I need to get this done."

Once upon a time, I thought our love would last forever.

The parachuting accident had not changed his priorities. It had not changed our marriage, either. It had bought us time, and time was running out.

12 | 9'er Domestic

9'er domestic: Refers to a soldier's spouse

"Shaved or sliced? Hey lady, tell me how you want it."
I stared at the peach fuzz above his lip as he held a chunk of chicken in the air. Without saying a word, I turned and left. I abandoned my cart, with the strawberries and grapes Owen and Steve both adored, and hightailed it out of the grocery store. I had barely started driving when the tears came. I had no idea where I was going. It just had to be anywhere but here.

I pushed down hard on the gas and cranked the music as I drove down the highway that stretched between my home and the city. The tears didn't stop coming. I didn't care who saw me. I had reached the breaking point, the point of no return. I was done. My counsellor Beth and I had discussed this possibility—that one day it would just be too much.

"How long do you think you can go on like this?" she asked me.

"I don't know, really. I just keep hoping that he'll get it one day and things will change."

"Danielle, that's unlikely."

"I know, but I still love him, even though it's getting harder," I said.

"I know you do. But do you love yourself, too?"

And now I'd hit the limit. I could no longer wait for Steve to see me, to get plugged into our life together. I needed more from our marriage, more from the man I had given every single part of myself to since I was nineteen years old. I needed to put myself first. It was way overdue. I forced myself to focus on the road. I didn't care about the groceries sitting in the cart or the supper that was expected on the table. I just kept driving.

Before this, I'd started going out again—partying like I was in my twenties. The more Steve trained, the more I drank myself into oblivion. We were now galaxies apart. I no longer had the words nor the will, to make him see what he was losing. The weekend before, I had gone out with my cousin and her friends, who had become my friends. While they drank and danced to blow off steam about the monotony of their work life, husbands, and kids, I drank to forget. The talk therapy helped me, but I still had countless layers of grief, anger, and loss caked to my ribcage.

Late one night, as our bodies bumped against strangers on the dance floor and strobe lights flashed against our faces, an arm grabbed me and pulled me in. I felt his shirt damp with sweat as I wrapped my arm around his back without hesitation. I let the music carry me while my head spun from too many tequila shots. The man brought me in closer, his jaw against my cheek, his hot breath against my neck. I tried to lose myself in the music, but my head started to clear as memories of Steve's body against mine overwhelmed me. My knees buckled and I lost my balance. The man brought me in closer, pressing himself into me, the music vibrating against our limbs. My cheeks were suddenly wet with tears, even though I hadn't felt them fall. My thoughts flashed to the day in our living room, when Steve sang in my ear as he squeezed me against his body so lovingly. How we moved across our living room floor barefoot while the afternoon sun poured in. How he pulled back, looked into my eyes, and told me that he loved me. "We're meant for each other, Dan." A hand was now touching the small of my back and all I could think of was that this guy was not the one. I would never dance with the one again. Even though I believed my husband did not love me anymore, I only wanted to dance with him.

We had fallen so far.

"What's your name?" the man hollered as I scrambled away before the song ended, wiping my tears. I left the bar after finding my cousin and telling her I wanted to leave.

During the half-hour cab ride back home, I convinced myself that I was going to tell Steve the truth. That I was dying inside. That I couldn't grieve in secret anymore. That I hungered for intimacy. That I was worthy of love. I wanted him to say that he would meet me halfway, that our love would conquer all. I wanted to hear these words more than anything.

I locked the door behind me, tore my clothes off, and crawled into bed. Steve sighed loudly, letting me know he was annoyed. It was after 1:00 am. I wept as I shifted to find a comfortable position in my single bed with the line in the middle. I didn't care that he could hear me. I wanted him to hear me. I crept towards the line that divided us. I knew it wasn't a good time to talk, but there never was a good time. He was always too busy or on his way somewhere. Always anywhere but here. Besides, I had truth serum pouring through my veins: five shots of tequila and four beers, at my last count.

"Go sleep downstairs," he said, without any concern in his voice.

"Steve," I said, "I really need to talk to you. Please."

"I mean it, Dan. You reek of booze and I have to get up early. Just go."

I sighed even louder than he had and heaved myself out of bed, grabbing my pillow, and ambled to the downstairs bedroom. My head was still spinning. I climbed into our old sleigh bed, where we had once slept with no gap between us and had made love. I tossed every pillow off of the bed and eventually fell asleep, overcome with sadness, the alcohol pulsing through my veins.

This was not the life I had planned. Of course, I never wanted a broken marriage, like the one I grew up in. I didn't want that for my son. My biggest fear when I said yes to Steve's proposal was that I might fail at it. And now I had.

I drove around, looking for answers, avoiding my husband and son. Without planning it, I ended up at my childhood home, a white two-storey duplex on the other side of town. This was the house where my parents' marriage had deteriorated, where alcoholism stole my innocence, where I lost my virginity, and where violence made me doubt everything. This was the house where I began to despise my father and question my mother. The one that smelled of Miller and cigarettes, where I learned to settle for crumbs of love. The one where porn was left in our upstairs bathroom, an irrational comparison to my thirteen-year-old body. Where my father walked in and walked out, until he walked out for good, and where I convinced my mother that life was worth living and could she please just eat a little.

This was the house where I learned to be a fighter, a protector, the person who said *go fuck yourself.* I thought about what Beth had said during one of our sessions. How there had been patterns in my life.

"You don't get anywhere overnight," she said. "Good or bad."

Passing the house, I drove downtown, towards my grandmother's house, my mother's mother, my sweet mémère. This was the house where she babysat me, after my mom went back to work. The one that smelled of *la soupe orange* and *gruau* hot coffee, and unconditional love. The house that gushed with stories, strength, prayer, and loss. The beacon that restored my innocence and that offered me respite without judgement.

I spotted Mémère as I drove by, sweeping her front veranda, a blue handkerchief tied around her head. Sorrow struck me again as I gripped the steering wheel and made the turn. I knew I would lose her someday, too, and no matter what, it would always be too soon. My heart could not bear to even think it. I pushed against the accelerator and kept driving.

I drove to the cemetery where Cindy, my friend, was laid to rest when we were both just sixteen. She was with me the night I looked out my bedroom window and saw my father in the arms of another woman. She had walked with me in the dark around my neighbourhood, consoling me, her arm firmly around my shoulders. I remembered her perfect smile and sparkling blue eyes and wondered where she would be today, and if we'd still be friends, if her life hadn't tragically ended in a car wrapped around a pole. I wanted to believe she was still with me, still by my side, holding me up.

The dash clock said I had been gone three hours. I was on the other edge of town and needed to get home. But something in me had snapped that morning and could not be repaired—the levee could no longer regulate the levels; the waters rushed all around me.

As I drove towards the suburbs, I made a promise to myself. I would leave as soon as the Paralympics were over. I didn't want to be the reason Steve didn't compete as well as he could have. I didn't want him to hold that over my head, too. I had to keep it from him until then. I was already committed to going to Beijing; the plane ticket was bought. This trip would be my final duty as his wife. After that, I would pick up the pieces of my life and learn to make myself happy again. Maybe even for the first time.

"Where were you all day?" Steve asked when I got home.

"Driving."

"I tried calling. You could have let me know. I was hoping to get some time on the water this afternoon."

"Sorry, I totally lost track."

"I thought you were getting groceries?"

"I'll get them tomorrow. I'll make supper now."

"Whatever. I'm going to my office. Owen is at the neighbours', playing."

I went into the kitchen and opened the fridge door, biting hard on my lip. Supper was on the table less than an hour later. The following afternoon, the fridge was fully stocked.

I'd made the decision and I was sticking to it, but how to tell Steve when the time was right? How to tell our family? Our friends?

"I know what everyone will think. That I couldn't accept him because of his paralysis."

"But what's the truth here?" asked Beth.

"It doesn't matter. Who leaves a man in a wheelchair? A *veteran*," I said, chewing my nails.

"Danielle, take a breath. Tell me what the truth is."

"That I feel like I do accept him, but he can't accept me. That I need more time to grieve, and he won't allow it. He won't let me feel it all," I said, kicking the legs of the coffee table. "I can't exist in the box he wants me to occupy. I can't live with the constant disappointment in his eyes. It's killing me."

"You know the difference, no matter what anyone thinks or doesn't think."

"I know, but I'm the one who looks like the asshole. The neighbours are one thing, but the thought of dealing with family is another story. His parents will despise me, his brother, his sister—even though we're not close."

"You've just solved another problem," said Beth. "Don't give any weight to the relationships you don't value. Name three people you really care about who will be affected by this separation."

"Steve, Owen, and my mom."

"Okay. Let's focus on these three people."

While I was planning my exit, my great escape from the only man I ever truly loved, Steve was planning for his world-stage challenge: the single-scull one-kilometre race at the 2008 Beijing Paralympics. Every morning, he woke up at 4:00 so he could be on the water by 5:30 and train. His day was filled with classes and schoolwork, and after school he spent time at the gym or back on the water. Weekends were filled with more training and competitions that took him away or boundless opportunities for him to speak publicly about his triumphant attitude and fighting spirit. He was already a winner, an inspiration, an absolute superhuman, respected and admired. His face had become a constant in the local newspapers. Every turn I made, I saw his photo, his story, his astounding success. Owen and I were pushed to the very back of his life, once again, forced to eat suppers alone. Sure, he asked us to come by the lake and watch him train so we could be "together," but I could no longer stomach it. I continued to raise my son alone.

"Hi, Danielle! Oh! Thank God the bus is late. I just made it back from town," she said with her toddler wobbling at her legs. "Stay here, Paige. So, how are you? I keep seeing Steve everywhere. You must be so proud of him, he's famous!"

"Yup, he's a superstar all right."

"So, is he excited? You're going to Beijing, right? You guys are so amazing."

"Uh, yes, I'll be there. Got my ticket."

"I have to admit, whenever I'm having a bad day, I think of Steve and you, and I give myself a little pep talk. You guys are crazy-inspiring."

"Wow. That's really nice, Shauna—"

"There's the bus. Look at the bus, Paige," she said, clapping her hands.

I couldn't go anywhere without people stuffing me with praise about my incredible husband. I wanted to tell them the truth, that he was a hero all right, but that he loved me not—that I was the hole in his bucket. Instead, I played the role of the good wife and gave them my million-dollar smile. This constant chipping away at my soul only reinforced my decision. I was done selling myself out. The clock was ticking.

I don't think Steve really noticed I was done until it was too late. His commitments, interviews, and training became all-consuming. It was heart-wrenching because, on the outside looking in, I was still proud of him—a starry-eyed fan impressed by his accomplishments and his ability to soar in all aspects of his life. But on the inside looking out, I felt betrayed. Unappreciated. Unimportant. Unlovable. And forever unable to measure up to his expectations.

"Steve, have you seen my keys?" I asked as I sprinted from one room to the next, combing every possible surface.

"Nope."

"Well, can you help me find them? I'm going to be late for the beading class."

"You never put your shit away. Just hang them on the hook. It's not hard."

"I don't need you to patronize me, I need your help. For God's sake, is that too much to ask? After everything I do for you?"

"You know, Dan, I've been thinking. The only time I feel shitty is when I'm around you," he said, now facing the kitchen.

"Well, maybe it's because I'm the only one on the planet not flying my freak flag for Steve Daniel. Sorry for not making you feel like a winner at home, Your Grace," I said, retrieving my keys from the wicker basket I had already looked in twice.

"You're crazy—like, nut-job crazy. You and your counsellor belong together," he said.

"Sorry for ruining your life, Steve." I grabbed my purse and left. His words lingered above me, filling the entire car as I drove into town. I continued to say nothing about my planned exodus. I spilled nothing except with Beth. It was only in her office that I let it out in bombastic chunks of agony.

"So are you sure you have everything?" I asked.

"I think I do," he said.

"Message me if you forgot anything and I'll pack it in my suitcase."

"So you're still coming?"

"Of course. I told you I'd be there."

"I know, but—"

"Owen, come and say bye to Daddy. Remember, we have something special to give him."

The sound of his pitter-pattering little socked feet flooded the hall. He looked so proud as he waited for me to give him the scrapbook I had made for his dad. My last love letter.

"What's this?" Steve asked surprised.

"Just some messages and well-wishes from your family, friends, and neighbours. Pretty much everyone," I said. "It's a journal filled with good luck messages, quotes, and drawings, made by me and Owen."

"Dan, I'm—thank you. For everything," he said, his eyes getting watery.

I looked away. "Well, Owen, give your daddy a kiss and a good luck hug. We don't want him to miss his flight."

I watched as Owen climbed up and onto his lap, wrapping his arms around his father's neck, resting his head against his dad's. My heart cracked. I kissed Steve's cheek and patted his back.

"Now, go kick some Paralympic ass."

He paused before he rolled out into the garage.

"Dan, thank you for this," he said. "I'm really looking forward to reading it on the plane. I didn't think—"

"I'm glad," I said. "I'm happy I was able to keep it a secret until now."

Unlike all of the other times he had left, I didn't watch his car disappear. I closed the door and locked it. I leaned against the wall, ripped out the elastic from my hair, and let my hair fall onto my shoulders, rubbing my scalp with both hands. In the kitchen, I turned on the music and poured myself a glass of red wine.

"Let's get your trains out, Owen."

I started to picture a life alone. With every day that passed, I felt better in my skin. I could breathe easier without the weight of pretending. But there was still so much to do before I left for China. And as much as I loved to travel, I did not look forward to being in Beijing. About six months after moving back to Sudbury, when things were better between us, when hope and optimism still shimmered, Steve and I had started the paperwork to adopt a little girl from China. After a few months into the process, we received an email from our adoption agency expressing their regret that China no longer allowed anyone with disabilities to adopt their daughters. We also had to make a combined $80,000 a year. In short, we were no longer "viable candidates for adoption." I hated China. I hated that they were hosting the Paralympics in China. That adoption experience was one more blow I'd had to absorb, one more thing that wasn't fair. As I crossed the days off on the calendar, I knew I'd have to suck it up one last time, on the world stage in a country I just wanted to give the bird to.

It was a long, lonely flight. Owen was with my in-laws, since my mom was teaching again. Nobody spoke any English from the time I landed at the Beijing airport. I managed to hail a taxi and pointed to the name of my hotel on my photocopied hotel confirmation. Thankfully, I arrived at the correct hotel where I met my new friend, Britt, the wife of another rower that I'd be sharing a room with. I slept until the following day.

Steve and I planned to meet near Athletes' Village. It was the day before his competition, so he couldn't venture far. I turned around and saw him wheeling towards me, a pale smile on his face. I watched him and smiled back weakly. Gone were the days when my heart would skip a beat and I could barely breathe waiting to greet and put my wanting arms around him. Confirmation. I was detached.

"*Ni hao*," he said, his eyes lighting up.

"Well, hello there."

"Welcome to Beijing." I awkwardly hugged him and patted his back. "So what do you think so far?"

"There's a lot of people in this part of the world," I said.

"Yeah, even more with the rest of the world coming to see the spectacle. Did you see me in the Opening Ceremonies?"

"I did catch of glimpse of you on CTV. Pretty cool."

"Well, I can't stay long, because I have a meeting with my coaches before dinner and then I have to get my head ready for the race."

"That's okay," I said, relieved that I wouldn't have to play a role any more that day.

"Let's take a stroll out this way," he said. I followed him.

The next day I took a forty-minute cab to the rowing event outside of the city. I passed dozens of poor neighbourhoods that had large white portable walls to hide the real China: poverty that littered the rural landscapes with garbage and laundry strung across the lands. I caught only snippets in between the white walls as the cab drove along the long highway. I wondered if that adoption would have changed us, made us stronger. I would never know.

During the race, I sat with other family members of the Canadian team, cheering heartily for Steve but at the same time struggling with the reality that my marriage would soon be over. He placed fourth in his heat and would race again the following day in the semi-finals.

Steve knew something was wrong when we first saw each other after his race.

"*Ni hao*! Great race," I said, greeting him in the family and friends tent.

"Thanks, but it would have been better if my oars had made it. Good old Air Canada. They broke them on the flight."

"You never told me that. That's insane! I'm so sorry. Well, I think you did great. You haven't been doing this for very long, remember?"

"I guess so," he said, puffing out his cheeks. "The semi-finals will be tomorrow afternoon. Hopefully I'll have a better race. So, what did you do today?"

"Britt and I went sightseeing. I think we ended up in a less touristy area. But the food was really good. Authentic. No McD's in sight," I said, avoiding his eyes.

"Something wrong?"

"Nothing really. Still trying to get used to the time difference."

"Yeah. I'm glad we got here early last week to acclimate to the time and heat."

"For sure."

"Dan, seriously, what's wrong? You seem different," he said, eyes wide and unblinking.

"Nothing."

"It is something. I can tell."

"It's not something I want to talk about here, Steve."

"Just tell me."

"I'd really rather not—"

"I don't care where we are, something is really off with you. What is it?" he said, sounding as if he were done pretending as well.

"I think we should talk about this when we get home. This is not the place and definitely not the time," I said.

His eyes filled quickly with tears. And then mine did. And I knew that he knew.

"We're not leaving until you tell me," he said.

"Geez. Fine. I, I just can't do this anymore. I'm done, Steve."

He glared at me. "Why did you even come here, then?"

"Because I said I would and I wasn't going to let you be alone in China. Nobody deserves that."

"You should have just stayed home. You're right. We'll talk about this later," he said as other athletes started to enter the tent.

I nodded.

"I'm heading back to the Athletes' Village to debrief the race and prepare for the next one. I guess I'll see you tomorrow?" he said with his sergeant's tone.

"Okay, I'll take a cab here and meet you after the race," I said, barely audible.

The next day, Steve finished his final race placing eleventh overall in the world in his arms-only single-scull category. He raced his heart out despite having borrowed ill-fitting oars from the Australian team. I saw him in the tent again, but other athletes and coaches surrounded him. I met several people as I tried to make my way towards him—yes, I'm Steve Daniel's wife, yes, so proud—shook their hands, and then left again for another night at the hotel. We didn't say anything to each other about the day before.

"I just want to get back to rest," he said, staring past me.

"Oh. Okay. I guess we'll see each other tomorrow, then?"

The following morning, he met me at the hotel. We had planned to spend two days together exploring the great city of Beijing.

"How has it been at Athletes' Village?" I asked.

"It's like Disney World for athletes. They're spoiling us rotten. You should see some of the athletes wolf down five Big Macs."

"What? Talk about healthy eating for high-performing athletes. So, do you still want to do this today? Tour the city?"

"I thought about it all night, Dan—what you said."

"You did?"

"The thing is, I haven't been happy for a long time, either. I think we should give this a try. Take a break, I mean."

"Oh. Okay, then," I said, a pang of sadness shooting across my heart.

"Yeah, I think that's what I wanted, too. I just didn't have the guts to say it out loud, like you."

I nodded.

"Let's just try to enjoy the city while we're here. We'll never be back again."

"That's for sure."

I pushed him up and down the great sites of the Forbidden City. We even attended an evening circus acrobat show with child gymnasts. We were on the edge of our seats all night as we worried about witnessing a spinal cord injury, making sick jokes that this was how China must recruit their Paralympic athletes. We were still a team when trying to summon a taxi. They wouldn't stop if they saw Steve in his wheelchair, so he hid while I hailed and then tried to explain using my hands that his chair broke down and we could get into his cab. Half a dozen drove away. Steve stopped me from causing any more of a scene as I yelled, "Mark my words, China, I will tell the truth about how you really treated the athletes during your precious Games!"

"You're going to get yourself locked up, Dan!" he said.

Even in our unravelling marriage, we were civil and kind. There was no attempt to change the outcome of our separation by either of us. When I look back on it now, I remember secretly hoping that he would beg me to stay, to make it work, to try one more time. I was hoping he would fight for me in that last hour. While we lay inches apart in our hotel room, the night before I left for Canadian soil, I listened all night long as he shifted and turned in his sleep, hoping he would reach out, put his arm around me, pull me in, and tell me everything I wanted to hear. That I was enough and he would do whatever it took to save our marriage. I wanted him to say, *Please don't go. It can't be over, not after everything we've been through.* But he didn't. He stayed on his side and I stayed on mine.

He was to visit in Beijing for another week with Team Canada to enjoy the rest of the Games and take part in the closing ceremonies. I was to go home and plot the next chapter of my life as a single mom.

"Well, they're calling a cab for me," I said.

"I hope you have a good flight back," he said, reaching for my hand, then changing his mind.

"Me too."

"Tell Owen I'll be bringing back all kinds of loot for him."

"I will," I said, my eyes tearing up.

"Okay, then. We'll talk about everything when I get back," he said.

"Yeah."

"I'm glad you came, even if—"

"Me too, it would have been weird not be to here to watch you race, after everything."

"For me, too."

"I'm proud of you—"

"Hey, Nico! You got in late last night," Steve said to his roommate, also a rower from Canada, while they did some kind of handshake. Nico was with his wife as well, the girl I had been touring Beijing with.

"My cab is here, Steve, I have to go."

"Okay," he said as I leaned in to hug him. He hugged me back as if I were one of his distant aunts. I held back my tears, pushing down the lump in my throat.

"Safe travels," he said as I turned toward the cab.

I stepped away, clutching my luggage handle for balance, and then fell into the back seat while the driver heaved my bag into the trunk. I looked back at Steve, praying, trying to will him to look back at me too. Just one last time—a morsel of intimacy still surviving. I watched him as he continued his conversation with his roommate, laughing, as I drove away from him and the city of twelve million people. He never looked back. Not even to wave goodbye. Not even after everything. I watched, my eyes fixed on him until he was just a speck.

13 | Military Issued

(Denoting possession and transfer of possession. Issued by the government.)

The last time I cried on a plane, I was leaving Steve in Paris. We had hopped from train to train across France, Italy, and Spain for three weeks while he was on leave from his Bosnia tour. Sitting on the metal chairs at the airport, he kept kissing my hand, my cheeks, my lips. Newlyweds after three years of marriage—we could thank the military for that, at least. We'd been apart so much that it was hardly as if we'd been married at all.

The final call came for my flight back to Canada. Steve was staying one more night in Paris and then he was heading back for four more months in Bosnia. I kept it together until the very end, until our fingers no longer touched. And then, the massive gate shouldering my emotions busted open, hinges and all. I gasped, throwing my head back as I tried to gulp down the boulder that was trapped in my windpipe. I couldn't breathe, the weight intolerable. I turned away from him, left him standing there as my heart shattered into a trillion pieces. I walked through the tunnel and onto the plane, where I anchored my body to 34A, grateful I had enough foresight to book a window seat for the way home. I wiped at the tears for eight hours, over the sea, until my Kleenexes became powder in my hands. I did not read, I did not whisper a single word to the woman squeezed against me.

Three days after Steve returned from Beijing, barely over the jetlag, I told him I was leaving. I had planned to wait a week before I brought it up. He was starting his third year of college and he'd already missed the first week of classes due to the Games. I thought I should give him a grace period, but the truth was, I couldn't live another minute without being real, not one more microsecond. Owen was already at school and Steve hadn't yet left for the day.

"I'm buying a house," I blurted.

Steve paused, binders and backpack in hand. "You're what?"

"I've been looking for apartments, but there aren't any two-bedrooms for less than a thousand a month that aren't roach motels," I said in my this-is-absolutely-non-negotiable voice.

"You've already looked?"

"Yes," I said. "This house is mine, too. I own equity."

"I know. I'm not going to fight you, Dan. I just didn't think you were scheming while I was gone," he said.

"A lot happened while you were training for the gold."

"Nice."

"This decision wasn't made overnight. It took me a year in therapy—"

"You and your damn therapy."

"I'll call the realtor tomorrow."

I viewed eight houses before I found the one I put an offer on, a one-and-a-half-storey yellow stucco house with mature trees lining the ridge of a small mountain in the backyard. The pickings were minimal and I was desperate to find a safe home for Owen. All the others were by train tacks or beside houses with permanent yard sales. This one was on a crescent and the neighbourhood felt safe. It was also close to downtown, where my bead store was located and closer to the college where I started teaching English, part-time. I won the bidding war and moved in one month later, in October. Steve bought me out of the house we owned together, and I used the money to purchase the new one. I also planned on using some of it as a cushion until the store made more money.

We continued to sleep in the same bed for three weeks—the line between us now an insurmountable barrier. I made supper for all three of us, but ate alone in my room. Steve barely said a word to me, our paths crossing only when they needed to. He spent more time in his office and climbed into bed only when I was already sleeping. I started picking up boxes and packing up my books and art supplies when Owen went to bed. I made lists of everything I had to do and places I had to call—hydro, gas, telephone companies. Steve had never before been the one left behind. This was new territory for the both of us.

We lied to Owen. We told him we'd be living in separate houses because I needed to live close to where I worked. Steve would stay in the big house and I would live in the small house. Owen would split his time in between both. He would go to the same school and I would drive him in and pick him up at the bus stop after school.

He was five.

He believed us.

The day I moved out, Owen was with my mom on Manitoulin Island. I didn't want the memory of our parting to sit with him forever, a nightmare where he watched his mother drive away with her belongings, away from the house he lived in. It was a sunny and cold autumn day. My boxes were packed but I left all the furniture, the kitchen appliances, and all of the pictures nailed to the wall. I wanted the house to look undisturbed, the same as always, for Owen.

Steve was home and seemed unbothered, almost jovial as he watched my brother, my best friend, Melanie, and her husband load the boxes into the U-Haul.

"Are you going somewhere?" Steve asked, grinning, as he watched us pile boxes into the truck.

"You're hilarious," I said. "A real comedian. You should take that show on the road."

After the first load was ready, I went to find Steve. He was in the bathroom.

"Hey," I said, knocking. "Can I come in?"

"Yeah, it's open."

"Are you okay?" I asked, letting a self-conscious smile slip across my face.

"Yeah," he said, echoing my awkward smile. "I knew it was coming. It's you I'm worried about."

"Me? What for? I never wanted this. I just can't live the way we've been living. And I don't want Owen to see the worst in us, which is what'll happen if I stay."

"Well, we both agree on that."

"Who knows," I said, "maybe we can be the next Demi Moore and Bruce Willis? They seem to be good friends despite going their own ways."

"You never know," he answered.

I didn't look back. I walked out the door and into the cold air, away from my suburban lifestyle, my status quo, my husband, my child, and my German shepherd. I drove to the new house and unloaded the boxes. My brother and Melanie's husband headed back to pick up the second and final load while I unpacked my books, my kitchen, and my bedroom.

It took only half the day to empty every box and arrange the little furniture I had brought with me. My old sleigh bed had been assembled, the one Steve and I had shared before the accident, before everything. I had the first couches we had purchased as a married couple, which had been sitting in the basement rec room. And the kitchen table. I didn't have any dishes, or a toaster, or even a kettle. I didn't have the heart to separate all the things that we had bought and built together, to be reminded of the memories that exemplified every single thing we had acquired in our ten years of marriage. Like the lime green dishes I adored from The Bay, the ones I had wanted so desperately. I had pleaded with Steve for twenty minutes, both of us standing in the aisle, my hands on my hips, and he finally gave in—a set of eight, just in case we broke some along the way. Now there were only six plates. I left them all.

My mom had an extra single-bed frame and mattress for Owen's room. I didn't have a dresser for his clothes, so I just hung them up. His room was pink but would soon become a fresh green. I wanted to make this room as special as the one he had in the big house. It was small but it had a lovely window that faced the falling leaves from the maples in the backyard. It also had a large closet that would make a brilliant cabin if I could get some lighting in there. I bought a red tool chest on wheels to store his toys and belongings. He thought it was cool to have his own red metal tool chest, like his dad.

I also got him fish, since our dog Molly stayed at the big house with Dad. She needed the fenced yard because she liked to run wild. I wasn't very good at taking care of fish. Orange Fish and Flipper only lasted two weeks. One morning, after a weekend of drinking, I sauntered into Owen's bedroom to feed them their stinky flecks of food, but it was too late. I scooped them out with the tiny red net and chucked their little bodies into the toilet. Plop, plop. I watched them swirl around the toilet bowl as I flushed them down into the void. Yet another disappointment I would have to narrate to my son. I felt horrible. And yet, I was also relieved that I didn't have to be responsible for them anymore.

In the beginning, being on my own felt like I no longer wore a mask. I had stopped counting the days, praying for a better one, day after day. I could breathe easier with no disappointed eyes on me, no more judgments—a whole new chapter was ahead of me and the sky was the limit. The honeymoon phase of the separation was euphoric. I felt brave. Strong. Independent. No one would hurt me again. I had stood up for myself, my self-respect.

I partied like it was 1999 for six whole weeks.

Steve and I split custody of Owen equally, without drama.

"Hey, how was your weekend, Owen?" Steve asked, rolling down his window as he came up one Sunday to get him.

"Hi, Daddy," Owen said, waving, carefully walking down the steps one at a time.

"Good," I said. "I took him to see the new *Madagascar* movie."

"Anything I need to know?" Steve asked, watching Owen climb into the truck.

"No, he's eating well and all systems are a go," I said.

"Good." He nodded, keeping his eyes on Owen.

"Yeah. Just let me give him one more kiss. Muah! I love you, Owen," I said, squishing his cheek with my mouth and trying not to let my voice tremble. "I'll see you soon."

"Bye, Mama," Owen said in a small voice.

"Okay, little man. Let's go," Steve said.

We were diplomatic. Courteous. This is the part I was most proud of, the way we respected each other after we were no longer legally married. (We had gone ahead with the legal separation; both of our lawyers had recommended it. "It's being smart," they told me.) We had spared Owen. We had freed him of knowing the pain that was caused when one parent speaks badly of the other. The pain that makes you question the good in yourself. I knew from experience the damage that caused.

I was fond of the cosiness of a small house; this one was about fifty years old. It had character, unlike the brand-new wheelchair accessible home we had built in the 'burbs. It had story. I loved the hard wooden floors that creaked under my feet in the morning, the sound of the furnace kicking in, the cerulean blue and lavender floral wallpaper in the pantry. I learned to love my retro bathroom, with its powder-blue toilet, tub, and sink. But Owen did not like coming to the small house. I'd pick him up at the bus stop three days out of five and take him away from the court where he played with his friends, away from the world he knew. It hurt me to acknowledge the pain I was causing him. The small house didn't have kids who played outside.

"It's not the same. Can't we stay here?"

"No, Owen. You know that Mama lives in the small house now," I said as I drove away, sucking back my tears. His dissatisfaction continued throughout the months. Even with the newly painted walls, his own mountain in the backyard, and the fish he had, for two whole weeks, he never felt at home.

"He's got a project to do this week," Steve said.

"Oh! Things are getting serious in kindergarten," I said. "I'm on it. What's it about?"

"The family tree," Steve said, like it was cancer.

"Oh. Okay," I said.

"Have fun with that," he said, letting his delight for the timing of this project sink into my skin like black ink. I grabbed Owen's bag from the back seat.

"I'll see you soon, li'l man. Daddy loves you."

"Bye, Daddy," Owen said, waving.

Owen was eating the same and sleeping the same. He seemed to be well-adjusted despite the occasional and quite normal request to stay in the big house when I picked him up. Steve and I were model single parents. Gold stars. His teacher even told us that she never would have known about the separation if I hadn't told her. Owen had shown no signs whatsoever. This was good, right?

By now, though, my drinking was out of hand. I'd drink a whole bottle of wine, getting smashed even before I left the house for a night of partying. It was my costume for the world I still did not fit in—a full-bodied, elegant blackcurrant fruit with a hint of spice and cedar and a dose of courage. When Owen was with Steve, I spent the nights around other drunk people. I had found another forlorn friend, recently separated and also a teacher. Together, we managed to forget our troubles, at least for a few hours every night.

As I stood at the bar, waiting to order another drink, a young man in a wheelchair went by. My body seized and I watched as he stopped to meet his friends, putting the brakes on his chair. I left the bar and hurried outside, into the open. My heart swelled with guilt. Memories. Him. Being so blitzed, I usually ended up in the smoking section bumming a cigarette off of someone I knew, or didn't know. This night was no exception. As I was lighting one, trying to shield it from the cold wind, I noticed a familiar hue of green to my right. A flicker. I moved in closer to make sure.

"Hey, what are you doing wearing that?" I asked, putting my hand on his shoulder. He was wearing a standard, military-issued combat jacket with a black toque and torn jeans. The same jacket Steve had worn to work every day for thirteen years. It was as if this guy had snatched it from our closet.

"What's your fucking problem?" he said.

"Where did you get that? You can't wear that here!"

"I can wear this anywhere, bitch. Free country and shit."

"It's not free, asshole. People die wearing that jacket and you're dishonouring it in a bar?"

"Let 'em die! Fuck the army. Fuck them all," he said pointing into the black sky.

I leapt toward him like a leopard about to swallow its prey in one gulp. I wanted to stop his mouth from spitting another word. Triggered like a pit bull by a green jacket with a maple leaf on its side. The thousand losses rising to the surface, drowning me.

"Danielle, leave that guy alone," my friend said, pulling on my arm. "He's nuts. Seriously, that guy is schizophrenic. Don't mess with him."

I spiralled out of the smoking crowd and walked home alone. It was cold and dark. I still did not fit in anywhere. I lived on the fringes. Half civilian, half military. Half single, half still married to a man who didn't love me enough.

As the snow continued to cover the ground, I found myself retreating again within my shell. The distance and time apart from the big house and the man who lived there with our only child was starting to creep into my thoughts and invade my days more and more. It didn't help that I saw his face almost weekly in the local newspapers—photos of him playing sledge hockey and basketball, and rowing. I thought for sure I would see him on the cover under the headline: "Sudbury's Newest Single." And then there was the spread about him winning the city's Community Builders Award. These glimpses of him felt like jagged little slices on the sides of my lungs.

"Still a winner, I see," I said, during another one of our hand-offs.

"Sorry?" he asked, narrowing his eyes as he craned his head in my direction.

"So are they giving you the key to the city now, too?"

"Oh that. Somebody nominated me," he said. "Okay, bud, Dad will see you soon."

I persisted despite this new source of pain I tried to conceal. His life still seemed full. Without me. He was succeeding and exceeding and moving on, just as he always had before. And as much as I wanted to move on, in every way, I hadn't—as always. I was actually starting to fall apart, like a chain repeatedly slipping off a bicycle. I wasn't getting anywhere. I just pushed the bike instead. Each passing day brought me closer to the reality that I was no Demi Moore to his Bruce Willis. Not even close. And what was worse, underneath all of the anger and resentment, beneath all of the collateral damage, I started to suspect I still loved him.

I wanted to skip Christmas and wake up in 2009. But I realized how selfish that was and decided to make it extra special, instead. Owen deserved it. I left his father and I felt I needed to make it up to him.

I went out and bought the tallest Christmas tree I could find. It was pre-lit and enormous, standing at seven and a half feet tall. It was ridiculous. I dragged it all the way to my car, twice. The first time I put it up, the lights didn't work. After yelling at the gods and bawling my eyes out and yelling at the gods again that they were not going to defeat me, that this was not a sign of things to come, I dismantled the tree and stuffed it back into the box. It didn't fit and I didn't care. I found a parking spot at the end of the snow-covered parking lot and dragged the box back into the store. Another woman with a similar box at her feet with branches poking out waited with me. It wasn't just me. I asked the woman wearing a red vest to open the new box with the new tree and watched her plug in the lights. They didn't work either. Damn you, Universe. The very patient and accommodating salesclerk offered to check the storeroom and found one last box. She checked the lights for me and then I dragged it out of the store and up the steps to the tiny house. I was going to get this tree up, no matter what.

I hung my generic, store-bought, memory-free decorations on my gargantuan tree. It covered most of the area of the dining room already crammed with a large piano I had let myself be talked into by the previous owners of the house. The tree was going to stay and it was going to be beautiful. I finished decorating it and fell into bed after midnight.

"We're not spoiling him just because we got separated," Steve said on the phone the next day. I had called him to discuss the dreaded Christmas holidays.

"I agree. I don't want to raise a spoiled brat," I said.

"Good."

"Why don't we keep the gifts simple and still from the both of us, just to make it easier?"

"All right," Steve said.

"So, how are things going at school?" I asked.

"I have to go," he said, and then the dial tone was ringing in my ear.

I hung up the phone, tears stinging my eyes.. *Well, at least we're still good parents.* I was relieved that a broken home didn't mean broken parenting, even though Steve disliked me so much. We had made a list together and the gifts were still going to be from Santa or from Mom and Dad, on the same tag. Solid co-parents. But not friends.

I continued to dread the holidays, especially when I saw families intact. Together at the movies, in restaurants. I wanted that again. I wanted that again with Steve, but I needed to be loved and accepted. I no longer wanted to love a lot and be loved a little. But I was starting to remember only the good times. My therapist said this often happens after a separation. The good times stick; the bad slip away.

Six weeks after I moved out, Steve still couldn't make eye contact with me during our Sunday afternoon hand-offs. I tried to get in there, to see if he still loved me. His poker face said nothing; he gave nothing away. As the snow accumulated, though, I realized there was still love rooting through, the way gardens can still come to life after the expiry of summer, fall, and winter. No matter how much snow falls, or for how long the vegetation is frozen, life sprouts again. My heart would not—could not—let him go. I started dreaming of him, of us together again, as a happy family. I would roll over in the morning and feel the cavernous ache in my chest as I stretched out to the other side of the bed.

By the first of December, the honeymoon phase of my separation was officially over. After waking up with another bad hangover, I rolled over and realized just how miserable I was. My heart was still broken. Independence, schmindependence. I recognized that I was alone with someone I still disliked—me, with my never-ending hangover, my anger and pain, my hair reeking of smoke, my green skin. And when I wasn't in this self-made purgatory, I was picking up my son for my three- or four-day quotas, feeling like the biggest piece of shit for splitting up our family. I tried to hide my guilt-ridden face and disguise my latest day after another horrible night out with an exaggerated smile when Owen opened the door to my car. But I knew he saw through that, too.

I worked long days at the store, getting it ready for Christmas. This was good. I spent each day sorting beads and cutting fabric and making art kits and handmade gifts for the holidays. We had painted the walls in jewel tones of pinks and golds and added two chandeliers. It looked like a very happy place and there was always so much to do, but there were too many days when hours passed slowly and my mind wandered. I mused about what Steve might be doing. Did he ever think of me? Would he ever forgive me? I didn't regret leaving. But I wasn't prepared for the aftermath.

I saw Beth less, anesthetising my pain rather than talking about it. The many books I had planned to read and the pages I had planned to write sat untouched. Even when I was finally free to feel it all, the way I had wanted to, needed to, while I was with Steve, I didn't bother. It all seemed like too much work after eating and washing and working all day. Instead, I turned to men; guys I would never have twice looked at started to seem like viable options. All I wanted was to fill the void. To make me forget.

To make me "unlove" him.

Eventually, I decided I needed to talk to Steve. I needed to know how he was feeling about things, if he now saw things as I needed him to, and if there was a chance for us to get back together or at least work towards reconciling. I had seen a photo of him in a local magazine with friends and a date at the Community Builders Award gala, for the award he had won. Seeing him with another woman made me realize that if we had any chance to reconcile, it would need to be soon, before someone else fell in love with him. Or worse, before he fell in love, too.

"Is everything okay?" my mom asked when I asked her to come and watch Owen.

"Yes. Not really. I need to talk to Steve. I just need to know if there's still a chance."

"He was a good husband in many ways—"

"Mom. Stop. I don't need to hear this right now."

"I'm just saying that maybe you rushed this. It's not like he ever cheated on you, hit you."

"Can you be here or not?" I asked, unwilling to explain how the standards had changed, that not cheating on or beating someone does not automatically make them good husbands. There was much more under the surface of our relationship that she hadn't seen. Plus, I knew she meant well.

I phoned Steve next. "Do you mind if I come by tonight?" I asked, pacing up the hall, squeezing the phone in my hand.

"No, Dan. For what?"

"I just want to talk."

"It's not a good idea. You made your decision."

"I'm just asking for fifteen minutes," I pleaded, my voice cracking.

"You're wasting your time."

But I went. The drive there was excruciating. It was dark and snowing. I prayed to be able to say the right words. I couldn't help but feel it was now or never. I parked the car and knocked on my old door. He opened it looking tired and sad.

"What's this about?" he asked defensively.

I knew by his tone that he was in no mood to talk and that I was truly not welcome. "I was just hoping we could talk. We haven't really spoken about it all since I left. It's been three months and I was hoping we could—"

"Talk about what, exactly? If this has anything to do with you wanting to come back, you can forget it. We're done. You made sure of that when you bought that house."

"Steve, please. I just need you to hear me out," I said, crying.

"Dan, I mean it. It's over. I've moved on and so should you."

"But—"

"Owen is my number one priority and that's all that matters to me right now. I just want to be a good father. But you and I are through. Do you understand me?" he said, his fists clenched in his lap.

My feet started to sweat in my winter boots. His eyes said it all, even more than the words he spoke: calm, cutting anger, an impenetrable resistance. I could feel it as I stood there and he sat in his metal chair as if it were a throne. I felt like a minion trying to get close to his robe.

I stepped out the door, backwards. Pushed out into the cold.

Banished.

Several months after he retired, the army sent Steve a framed Certificate of Service in honour of his fourteen years in the military. I thought about creating a similar framed certificate for serving as a military wife, the dependent, and hanging it above my bed as a reminder to look ahead, just like him:

*In recognition for time served, solo child-rearing, dreams put on hold,
untapped professional and personal development, and countless
emotional damages. On behalf of the Government of Canada, we thank
you for your faithful and devoted service to your husband. Please
note your services are no longer required. You are asking for more than
he is willing and able to give. There is no compromising in the
Canadian Armed Forces. (You should have moved on, like he told you.)
Your contract is now terminated.*
Pro Patria

My mom was peeking through the blind as I drove up the driveway.
When she opened the door, I collapsed into her arms.

"We're done, Mom," I wailed. "He wants nothing to do with me.
Told me to move on."

She held me while I sobbed. I knew she understood this pain. My
father had said the same to her.

On Christmas Eve, I went to the big house as a guest. Steve's parents
and his brother and wife were already there with their kids. I walked in
as they were opening their gifts. I felt like an alien; it was awkward for
them and for me. But everyone did their best to act cordial. Steve had
agreed to let me sleep there so we could both wake up with our son on
Christmas Day.

"Don't think this will happen every Christmas," he said.

His family did not stay long after the gifts were unwrapped.
Pleasantries were exchanged and they closed the door behind them.

After bathing Owen and getting him ready for bed, I prepared my
own bed on the couch and left the Christmas lights on. I had put up
the tree a few weeks before because I didn't want them to go without a
tree. I lay on my old couch like a stranger, thinking of the family I had
torn apart when all I wanted to do was fix our lives. I closed my eyes
and pressed my hands over my heart, as if to contain such engulfing
sorrow. I missed my family. I tried to get comfortable as I stared at the
naked shelves that used to hold my books. I gave up trying to sleep and
knocked on Steve's door and let myself in. I offered my body and he
took it. But he wanted nothing else.

The next morning we were gold star parents again, unwrapping
gifts with Owen. I had gotten Steve a little something, an ornament
that meant courage in Mandarin. I thought it was perfect—small but

thoughtful, referencing his Paralympic Games in Beijing the summer before. I also bought him Barack Obama's biography. He was touched by the gifts, I could tell. He gave me some Yves Saint Laurent soaps, their Christmas scent. At least it was something.

After we opened our presents, Owen and I got ready to go my mémère's. It was a tradition we had followed my whole life and it was strange to go without Steve.

"Um, do you want to come, to my grandmother's place?"

"Thanks, but I'll pass. I'm just going to stay and play video games. My brother should be coming back at some point today."

"All right," I said, disappointed.

"Listen, nothing's changed," he said, locking his eyes on mine. Owen had gone to use the bathroom before putting on his winter gear.

"Oh. Okay." I leaned against the door, the cold glass pressing against my back.

Steve's ability to detach was second to none. He had perfected it. Even though I knew where it was coming from, why he was able to erect such a cruel and heartless wall, it hurt just the same. A few years after we had started dating, Steve had opened up about his mother.

She had him at seventeen, and Steve's earliest memories were of her unremitting threats of abandonment if he didn't stop crying or misbehaving. I suspect there were many valid reasons why she was unable to cope—raising a brown boy as a white mother in a northern mining town in the '70s, knowing only limited English, having recently immigrated from Finland, with barely any support, and of course still being a child herself. But I knew for certain her words had marked him, hardened him, and made him capable of loving only a little. He could never fully open his heart; his fears always shielded him.

"My mother and I have never been close," he said to me so many years ago. "Something has always been in the way. It's made me hard," he said, while his head lay in my lap, his eyes locked on the ceiling.

Maybe that's why the army was always number one. The army was the only family that made him feel secure, confident. The only family that would never abandon him—no man left behind.

But in the end, they did, too.

In my vulnerable and dejected state, with my body and heart seeping with despair, I understood why Steve was so incensed with me. When I was young, I really believed I could break through the blockade wrapped around his heart; I naively thought I could undo the damage. In the end, I did the one thing he feared most. The one thing he believed the army would never do. I had left him.

Steve came to pick up Owen on December 27 for a stay until New Year's Day. I loaded his truck with all the toys my family had gifted. I kept the smaller things at my house and the larger ones were sent to the bigger house. No wonder he never liked the small house.

I had no plans for New Year's Eve. And after I sent my son with his father and his big toys, I started my huge descent to rock bottom.

The drinking was getting old. The bar hopping was done. The red wine was no longer deadening the pain, even temporarily. I lay on the couch for five days and five nights. I watched TV and slept. Ate chocolate and called no one. Except Steve. I called him New Year's Eve around 6:00 in the evening, crying. Sick of myself and so goddamn lonely, I just couldn't stand it anymore.

"Hey."

"What's wrong," he asked right away.

"I—I uh, just needed to call you."

"Okay," he said, sounding compassionate for the first time since I had moved out. "What's going on, Dan? What's wrong?"

"Nothing. Everything. I'm just so sad, you know? It's so hard. It's just the time of year, and with everything else…" I sobbed into the phone.

"What are you doing tonight?" he asked.

"Nothing. Absolutely nothing. I just want to stay home."

"Why don't you call your friend Melanie or Julie? Please call them," he said.

"Yeah. I just don't know what to do anymore, you know? My heart just can't take any more pain."

"I'm worried about you," he said.

"I don't know where to put all this pain, Steve. I thought this separation was the answer. I really did."

"I'll call you tomorrow," he said. "But please call one of your friends or your mom tonight. Or call me back, if you need to."

I hung up the phone and emptied my debilitated heart, scraping the very bottom of everything that had happened in the last year. I woke up on the couch at 10:00 and continued to watch the New York City New Year celebrations on TV. I fell asleep before the ball dropped.

I woke up the next morning to the sound of loud knocking at the door. It was my mom, looking worried.

"I've been trying to call you for two days."

"My cell is dead and I can't find the cordless."

She was surprised by the mess. I usually kept the small house so tidy. Instead, empty chocolate and chips bags and bottles of wine littered the floor and tabletop.

"You should go take a shower. I'll clean up in here," she said.

"I don't know what to do, Mom. Where do I go from here? All I ever wanted was for him to love me," I said, my hand against my heart.

"I know, sweetheart. I know. Go take a shower and we'll go from there."

I took the longest, hottest shower I've ever taken.

I washed off all of 2008.

14 | Sitrep

It was my fifth day in a row on the treadmill. The dark winter morning still hung as I thumped against the hard rubber belt, earbuds bellowing music in my ears while other early risers ran beside me. The YMCA was a ten-minute drive from my house and I had finally made a promise to myself to get healthy again. For me.

On January 2, I committed to a 5K, a local race taking place in May, by signing up online and paying the fee. I ran and pushed through each difficult stride, and even though I was running in place, I was getting somewhere. I was moving further away from the person I once was and closer to the one I wanted to be. It wasn't easy getting up in the dark, in -30C weather, and putting on my running shoes. But I did. There were no other distractions while I ran on the treadmill but my own thoughts. I shed more than pounds while I trained for the run.

Under the pummelling of my feet, I could feel the anger thinning.

Turning the page to a new year on the calendar made me want to start anew. I wanted to treat my body with kindness, on all levels. It had carried me so far, even with all of the pain and torment. I was still standing. It was time for change.

My drinking days now were few and far between. I was determined to face the pain head on and to work through it, for good, and was resolute in caring for myself the way I had cared for everyone else, for years. The nights without Owen had previously hummed with the sound of the TV to fill the emptiness. But it only filled my little house with hollow echoes. I turned it off and started reading again. I surrounded myself with books and read them cover to cover instead of emptying bottles of wine. I lost myself in the worlds of others and began to see myself within their splintered lives. I roamed bookstores and libraries; each colourful spine called me. I wanted to touch them, inhale them, and stitch words to the inside of my skin. I slept with books by my side, rolling over them in the night. Books were the first things I touched every morning. I would not leave the house without one or two in my bag. They had become my new lifeline.

The voracious reading brought back my appetite for the written word and the stories that made me feel like I wasn't alone. I read memoirs like *The Glass Castle* and *The Year of Magical Thinking*, and I reread *Reading Lolita in Tehran*. I began to think about my own writing again, about how a professor in my Women in Religion class in university had encouraged me in my third year. We had been asked to write three essays; one had to be about a personal experience that had changed us. "You might consider writing for a living," she wrote in red pen at the bottom of my paper, a story I had shared about my childhood. "It could be healing for you and for others who read it." Her words, even then, were marks I was tallying on my scale, the one trying to tip me away from the damage done. I carried this paper in my backpack for months with the red "A" slashed across the top right corner and her tiny words scribbled at the bottom. I thought about the stories I had already written a few years before about our life in the military, and especially the one about the day that changed everything. I wanted to write again, to scratch my pen against the paper and let the words carry me into the places I had feared to go for so long. The nudge to write soon became more of a shove—a call to action. It would sporadically wake me in the middle of the night, summoning me to get the stories out. I moved a small table into the corner of my bedroom and started writing by hand in a large journal.

Every time I sat, the words poured out.

Maybe it was because we were no longer living in the same house or maybe it was just time, but I was finally able to write about Danielle and Steve in a way that moved me forward, to a new place.

I joined a local writer's group. We met every Friday night at the local *Fromagerie*. I sipped tea and sat among eight to ten other people who cared about the written word as much as I did. It didn't matter that most of them wrote Sci-Fi; it was a commitment I had made to myself, and one that I kept. Friday nights were about gathering my writing tools, my written pages from the week, and no longer deadening my body with booze. Those days were over.

I also enrolled in a group meditation class, adding to my growing list of self-care activities. My cousin, who was also my business partner, was fundamentally changed after her six weeks in this course, so I decided to take it up too. The intent was to clear emotional and spiritual blockages to help you move forward in your life. I was nervous at first. I knew I'd have to be present, and I wouldn't have any wine or books to shield me from what would surface. The class was two days a week, on Tuesday nights and Sunday afternoons.

The first time I went, I was the first to arrive. I chose a spot on the left side of the room, by the heavy-curtained window. Several women soon followed, each different from the one before. They were young and old, from their early twenties to their early seventies, dressed simply or ornately, with lots of jewellery. We sat in chairs in a circle in the small and dark room, all of us wanting to move on from something. I counted ten women, including the facilitator named Brennan, a small woman with long, red hair.

"Hello, dear ones. I'm so happy you have gathered here today and committed to this experience together. I have taught this specific class several times now and I'm amazed at the changes that take place."

"I'm ready," said a woman sitting to my left, with a deep scratchy voice. "I don't want to carry this crap around anymore."

"Well, you're in the right place," Brennan said as I shifted my feet under my chair. "Let's get started, shall we? Let's close our eyes and take three deep breaths in and out."

After breathing in and out just three times I could feel my head already begin to spin, my breaths had been so short and shallow that I wasn't used to so much oxygen rushing up to my brain. I let myself be carried by her words as she brought us deep inside our bodies. We travelled into ourselves, past our blood and our bones and into the place far beyond. Into the stillness.

"Now that we have arrived at this profound place, I want you to scan your body from the very top of your head to the tip of your toes. I want you to skim over every part, feeling for any uneasiness or heaviness. If you do feel a block, I want you to wash it away with a warm, white light. Infuse it with your healing glow until you feel it is no longer a shadow."

After the first night, I could barely drive home. My body was so tired and unaccustomed to being in such a state of tranquility. I climbed into bed and tumbled into a bottomless slumber.

We were encouraged to continue our "light work" during the week and make notes of any changes we were experiencing, good or bad. I looked forward to the second session. However, during the third, I reached the core of my pain, having gone deeper and deeper, like opening one babushka doll after another until I reached the pea-sized doll that held the magnitude of my wreckage—the space where I stored my sorrow. I sat with the burden of my broken heart in a room with nine other women, and I wept uncontrollably.

"Oh, sweetie, I know this isn't easy. But you're safe here and you're not alone. We're all here sending you love as you repair your vessel," Brennan said.

I couldn't stop crying. There was no more sucking it up. No more pretending behind the booze, the faux smiles, the lies I wore as I bought milk and bread. At last, I sat in silence, refusing to run from the deep and painful purging of the years of muck I had been carrying like sandbags attached to my body; all of the grief I couldn't access when I was living with Steve and was not permitted to take the time I needed to heal; the grief that alcohol could not mask or even help me access long enough for me to mend it when I was finally on my own.

After completing the third week of group meditation, I abandoned work in the middle of the day because the tears would not stop. It was a Friday afternoon and my cousin and I usually worked in the shop together on Fridays. We called it Fun Friday, when both our sewing machines would buzz as we worked to fill the shelves with aprons, tea cozies, and pencil cases.

"Danielle, what's wrong?" Julie asked.

"I just can't stop. It's like a tap that won't turn off," I said, wiping my face with the polka-dotted scrap fabric sitting on the table.

"I know. That class does something to you. It brings you to the source—a wild trip." I nodded. "Just go home," Julie said kindly. "This is not Fun Friday for you. Go home and don't even think of this place."

For two whole days I wept. I cried until there wasn't a tear left in me.

Week after week, with my new healthy strategies, I continued to expel the animosity and resentment I had accumulated during my marriage. I also began to face the anger I felt towards myself. I knew I wasn't perfect and I began to own my part and see the patterns—the one where I was never happy, even before the accident, before the army, and before Steve. I admitted that I had brought this unhappiness into the marriage.

I went to these unmapped places and uncovered the reasons for this long-lasting misery, this lack of self-worth, and the ways I contributed to the demise of our relationship. I was wounded long before I started loving Steve. Deeply wounded. The paralysis, military life, the loss of our first child—while they were all truly heartbreaking in their own ways, they also became diversions I used to avoid looking at my other, personal pain—all of my previously broken bits. It was so much easier to blame everyone and everything else—that is, until I was completely alone. Things became crystal clear when I had only a mirror to look into, when I became sober enough and alert enough to hear and see the truth.

Through this painful process, I uncovered my need to work towards something that genuinely fulfilled me, that gave me a sense of purpose. Writing was the one thing that always came circling back. I knew writing would help pull me out of the dark trenches I had forged around myself for almost thirty-five years. I couldn't lie when I faced the white page.

I completed the six-week course feeling as though I had been overhauled. I had new eyes. I could see the good in Steve again. He was a loving father, a loyal man. Trustworthy. He had more determination and resilience than anyone I had ever met. I remembered the kind things he once did for me. How he stuck sweet notes to a dozen surfaces when I got back from the hospital after having Owen. *You are strong and beautiful* was pasted to the mirror in the bathroom; *for your pain, my love* was on the Extra Strength Advil bottle; *you'll feel better soon* was glued to my bag of sanitary pads under the sink, hearts drawn around his words.

We had loved each other fiercely once.

The space and time to grieve, and the ability to go inside my ruined heart, allowed me to finally start to heal, more than I had during my one-hour sessions with my counsellor, Beth. Her support was vital then, but I could barely scratch the surface before I'd have to bottle it up again and return home, wearing my grief as a wall, separating myself from Steve and the world. I now allowed myself to feel it all as it surfaced, while I wrote or ran on the treadmill. I could sit inside the many losses that arose while I read late into the night, in the silence. I permitted the pain from inside my body to bleed through my breathing space and stain the empty pages of my journals as I wrote longhand at my table. I no longer walked the streets with a clenched jaw, or combed the bars with a devastated heart. I didn't even hide the tears from Owen anymore.

"What's wrong, Mama?" he asked as we played with playdough in the living room.

"I just feel sad, Owen," I said, as he looked at me, uneasy. "And sometimes, when you're sad, you cry."

He hugged me tightly with his small arms around my neck, his head pushed against my chest.

I began to see myself as doing the best I could as a human, flawed, and still worthy of love. I began to think of Steve as a boy, of his earliest memories of abandonment and fear, of him growing up as the only brown boy in his high school, in the whole town, forced to prove his worth again and again in an imperfect world, always doing his best in extremely arduous circumstances. He rose, over and over, triumphant, despite all of the odds against him. After two months of consistent meditation, running, reading, and writing, I discovered that I truly still loved him, flaws and all. And above all else, I truly loved myself, too.

I had *finally* found my new beginning.

15 | Rendezvous Point

It was early March and the snow was melting quickly. Owen and I waited outside the small house for Steve to arrive. We splashed through the puddles as Steve pulled up towards us. He was wearing his sunglasses but pushed them up on top of his head as we approached his truck.

"Beautiful, sunny day," he said, his bare arm hanging out the window.

"It sure is, especially when you get to jump in puddles," I said, letting myself dance with Owen one last time, squeezing his hands in mine.

Steve smiled, looking at us.

"Thanks for helping Owen with that family tree project," he said. "He got it back last week. I guess they hung it in his class for a while."

"Oh. No worries. We had fun cutting and gluing," I said, blowing my bangs out of my face.

"It looked great," he said. "You've always been good at that kind of thing, making it special, I mean."

"Thanks," I said, my cheeks flushing.

"I'll see you in a few days," he said with a light in his eye.

"Yes," I said. I waved goodbye to them both.

The following weekend, I planned on getting an early start on some spring cleaning. I called Steve to ask him a favour.

"Hey, what are you doing today?" I asked.

"Not much, I have a paper due Monday."

"Do you think I could use the garage to clean my car? I'm in full spring cleaning mode."

"Uh, sure. I'll move mine out. Just so you know, Owen's at a birthday party for the afternoon."

"Okay, thanks. I'll be there in an hour."

I drove into the garage and started right away. Steve had lined up the cleaning supplies on the small table with a few rags and a bucket. His garage was meticulous, as always. It made me grin to see everything so neat and organized.

As I was washing the inside of my car, he came into the garage.

"How's it going?" he asked.

"Good. Just finishing the inside now."

"You missed a spot," he joked.

"Funny one," I said, remembering how unfunny his jokes always were, even though he always tried to convince me otherwise. "I'm sure it's not up to your standards, but it's a definite improvement," I said, teasing him with the rag.

"It looks good. So, I was just about to make some lunch. Did you want to come in?"

"Yeah, sure. That would be great."

We ate our scrambled eggs and toast sitting across from each other at the small table he used to prepare food. Our knees almost touching.

"So what's new these days?" Steve asked.

"Well, lots, actually."

He smiled curiously.

"I signed up for the 5K happening in May."

"Wow. Good for you."

"Yeah, it has been. I've been going to the Y, like, four days a week and I'm really enjoying it, surprisingly."

"You seem different," he said.

"Different how?" I asked.

"I don't know. Less angry. Happy, even."

"I am. I've joined a meditation group and I'm writing again."

"You are? You did?"

"Yeah. I've been clearing a lot of junk."

Steve looked at me, bemused.

"I know you don't really believe in all that New Age stuff, but it's really working for me."

"Well, whatever it is, it's nice to see."

We continued to eat our lunch in silence. The radio was on, playing CBC in the background.

Finally, I broke the quiet. "Do you think maybe we'd be able to go out for supper one night, like on a date?"

"I don't know, Dan," Steve said, pushing around the egg on his plate. I held my breath and watched his hands. "Well, I guess we could."

"All right, then," I said, beaming at him.

"I can't promise you anything."

"I know, I know. Just dinner."

"Okay. Dinner. I'll call you," he said.

I continued to eat my scrambled eggs, even while my exhilaration buzzed right down to my toes.

Steve called two nights later. "Hey, it's me."

"Everything okay with Owen?"

"Yeah. Everything's fine. So, I was wondering if you still wanted to do dinner?"

"Of course," I said, dancing on the spot.

"All right, how's Friday at 7:00? I'll make a reservation at Verdicchio's."

"Sounds perfect," I said.

"Okay, then. We have a date."

"Yes, we do," I almost screeched before hanging up the phone.

I ran to my room and jumped on my bed, falling back on the pillows, imagining all kinds of romantic scenarios with the man I had known fifteen years. I darted to my closet and started raking through the choices. Not feeling like any of these outfits were viable picks for our first date, I grabbed my keys and headed to the mall.

I called my mom to tell her about our date.

"I'll babysit. I can take Owen to the Island. It gives you guys more time."

"It's just dinner, Mom."

"I know. But it's a start. I'm so happy for you, Dan. For you and Steve and Owen."

"Me too, but I need to know that he's changed, too. There's no way I can go back if he's still the same. We can't go back to before."

"I know. Just have a good time. I'll be praying for the most benevolent outcome."

"That's allowed," I said, laughing.

Steve and I dated four years before we married, but it was a long-distance relationship. I lived in residence at the University of Ottawa and he lived in the barracks in Petawawa. He visited me most weekends. We drank lots of beer and had lots of sex in those days, but there was no courtship—no dates where the boy picks up the girl in his truck and drops her off, kissing her goodnight.

This was different now. Special. I was going on a real date with my husband. I wanted to look perfect. He was taking me to the most expensive restaurant in the city and I had never been there before.

I must have checked my makeup and hair a dozen times while I paced up and down the narrow hall of my home. My hair was straightened, just touching my shoulders, and my lips glossy. I'd put my outfit together carefully: black pants and a sheer black blouse with just enough showing, finished off with my tall, black boots. I wanted to wear the gold and pearl necklace Steve had given me a year after we had started dating. I kept it in the jewellery box he had brought me back from Budapest made of cherry wood with beautiful carvings etched on all sides. I ran my fingers over the carefully engraved stars and flowers. Steve had called it a "secret jewellery box" because you had to follow certain steps to succeed in opening it. You had to push the sides and then the front to be able to retrieve the key. The left side of the box had a segment that slid forward and the key was tucked inside of it, snug in between two grooves. Steve had written a message on the inside of this wooden piece, in cursive, with a blue ballpoint pen: *"To Danielle ... the love of my life! Steven."* I slid the tiny key out of the grooves and unlocked the box and found the necklace, sitting in the far corner. Then I slid the chipped mirror, attached to the inside lid, revealing a cut hole, and reached in to find a letter Steve had written to me almost fifteen years ago. I read it, letting my heart fill, and then folded it and slipped it in my front pocket, leaving the necklace in the jewellery box and the key sitting beside it.

I peered out the window looking for his silver truck, doing deep breathing exercises and trying to shake out the nerves. I had a tendency to get my hopes up, and I knew I should try to ratchet down my expectations. We would both have to want this equally. There was no going backwards. Not after all this.

Turning the corner and driving ever so cautiously, he made his way up my long street. I took another deep breath and turned off the music and lights and quickly made my way down the steps. I smiled as he pulled up towards me. He looked good. He always looked good. He was wearing a blue button-down shirt under his navy blue leather bomber, and his hair was shorter than the last time I had seen him.

"Hello, there," I said. I got in the truck and breathed deeply. He smelled amazing, strong and sweet all at once.

"Hi," he said, letting a smile span his face, but quickly curling in his lips. I sat there as I had done hundreds of times before. But this time, I sat up straight with my legs and heels together, trying to make polite conversation without letting my nerves get the better of me.

"I spoke to Owen tonight. It sounds like he's having a good time with his cousins," I said.

"Well, that's good. He loves spending time with them."

"He does," I said, tapping the side of my leg. "So, what did you do today?"

"Studied, played video games."

"Sounds like a good balance," I said with a giggle.

"They're not the kind of games I want Owen to see. I play them only when he's gone."

"I appreciate that."

"What about you?"

I looked around his truck and realized he had probably cleaned it again, just for tonight. It was immaculate and it even had the new car smell, even though his truck was now four years old. I couldn't help but feel this was a good sign.

"So?"

"Oh, sorry," I said, chuckling. "I went for my workout at the Y this morning and then I just stayed home and cleaned and read. Typical Saturday off, these days."

"Are you still writing?"

"Yes, actually, and more so in the last month. I've also joined a writer's group."

"Sounds serious," he said. "You've been wanting to write for as long as I've known you."

"Yeah. I'm committed to finishing those stories I started so long ago."

"I'm happy to hear that, Dan. Really."

As we pulled up to the restaurant, we both searched the entrance for the wheelchair parking. There it is, I thought, but didn't say it out loud. Steve had disassembled his chair to fit it in the back seat. The weather was freezing.

"Just give me a minute to put the chair together," he said. "You can wait inside."

"No, that's okay." I said. My knees knocked and my teeth chattered as I watched him assemble his chair and transfer into it.

Inside, the waiters helped seat us at our table and lit the candle.

157

"This is fancy," I said.

"Yes, and the food is good, too. I came here a couple of months ago with Trish and Gordon when they were up from Edmonton." Gordon was Steve's oldest friend.

We both ordered a glass of wine. This is it, I thought.

The small talk continued for a while; we spoke about Owen and his school, the store, our dog, Molly, and Steve's classes at the college.

"You look very pretty," he said as we waited for our main course to arrive.

"Thanks," I said, trying not to let the warm blush burning my cheeks surface in the dimly lit room.

"I'm really glad to see you doing so well, with the running and the writing and everything. I get the feeling that you're in a much better place now."

"I am, Steve. What about you?" I said, pressing my feet into the floor. "Do you feel you've changed in the last five months?"

"Trying to make the most of it," he said. "Staying positive for the young fella, but I admit, it hasn't been easy."

He looked at me and held my gaze, and in that moment I knew he still loved me. It was the first time he had shown me any vulnerability. He was going to let me in.

"It's been lonely, Dan. Really lonely, but it's also given me time to think. About everything."

Our server arrived with the worst timing ever. We ate: steak and potatoes with roasted vegetables for me and oven-roasted chicken with seafood for him.

The coffee eventually came and we still had not gotten back to the conversation we'd started before dinner. Instead, I felt him pulling back as he cleared his throat and played with the cuff on his shirt. He scratched the top of his head as he often did, and in that moment I just wanted to disclose how much I still loved him and how I still believed more than ever that we were meant for each other. But I didn't.

"This is really nice," I said, adding milk and sugar to my coffee.

"Yes, it is," he answered, looking at me like he was deliberating his options.

I could still feel his shield, despite his willingness to have dinner together.

"Steve, do you think, you could, um, ever want to try and make this work again?"

"I don't know. I'm really not ready to go there. But this is a good start, don't you think?"

"Of course," I said, shuffling my feet under the table. "I never even expected us to be sitting here like this, at dinner."

"Me either," he said with a laugh.

"It's just, I've been hoping that we could work at this together. You know, give it one more try. I'm not asking to move back in."

"Let's not ruin a good night, okay? You know I'm not the kind of person to make any rash decisions. Especially now. Not when Owen is involved."

"We're on the same page when it comes to Owen," I said.

He put another sugar in his coffee. I moved my chair as close to the table as I could and went for it.

"Do you feel like we both needed this break? I mean, despite the fact that I was the one to walk away?"

"I'll admit it, Dan. Things couldn't have kept going the way they were. It would have gotten ugly. It was getting ugly. It's just," he said, avoiding my eyes, "I never thought you'd really ever leave. But you did," he said, now locking my eyes to his, showing me his pain, heartache.

"I did, and I can never take that back. But, I had to." He was still leaning forward, elbows on the table. "I needed you, too," I continued. "I was hurting and I wasn't able to tell you how much. You wanted to bury it and keep it all in the past. But I couldn't live like that anymore. It was killing me."

"Well, I guess it's just the way you did it. Buying a house. It was all so much and so fast after Beijing, and right before a new school year."

"I'll agree it did happen fast, but you and I both know this was brewing long before that. Before the accident even. And you always had something going on. There never would have been a good time." He was still listening. Still engaged. I kept going. "I just couldn't go one more day," I said, almost breathless now.

"I know, Dan, I've had a lot of time to think about it."

"And?" I asked, my hands now squeezing my cup of coffee.

"I know I was selfish—that I only cared about my goals. I know I never put you or our marriage first, and I'm so sorry for that. I wasn't hearing you, and I wasn't giving you what you needed."

My eyes started to well up, but I held back the tears.

"It wasn't fair, the way I treated you. You were always there for me, through it all: the tours, the accident, rehab. I know you loved me.

Nobody else could understand where I've been and where I am now. We've been through it all together," he said. "But I also know that you hurt me when you left. More than you will ever know. It will take time for me to let you in again."

"I understand," I said. "I never wanted to hurt you. I just didn't know what else to do."

"I know that now."

"Steve—"

"I took you for granted Dan. Distance has a way of helping you see things."

"It wasn't just you," I said. "I understand now why you had to move forward and keep filling your days. I know you did what you had to, to survive this. We're just so different and we had to deal with the loss in our own ways. I think we both did the best we could, even though we both really hurt each other."

"I'm just asking you to be patient with me," he said.

"I can do that," I said. "I can totally do that."

"I still love you," he said as he reached over and grabbed my hand.

"I love you, too. I've always loved you," I said, my lips quivering, tears now filling my eyes.

"So we'll take it slow," he said.

"Slow," I said, squeezing his hand.

When we left, snow was falling thickly. He pulled into the driveway and put the truck in park. For a minute, we watched the snow build up and slide down the windshield.

"I'm really happy we did this," I said. "I wasn't sure what to expect tonight."

"I feel the same way," he said, reaching again for my hand. My head a little dizzy from the wine and my stomach hummed with anticipation.

"It was more than what I had imagined. But I do tend to keep my hopes in check," he said.

"Yes, we're opposites in that way," I said, smiling, cautious.

And then he leaned in and kissed me. His full lips touched mine, soft and gentle, as if it were our first kiss, but also as if no time had passed between us—like the past, present, and future were happening all at once.

"I've missed that," he said.

His kiss was the only one that ever mattered.

We agreed to take it slow, but before too long we were talking on the phone every day. We went on a couple of movie dates and coffee dates, just the two of us. Then I started to go to the house for dinner and movie nights—the three of us together. I always travelled back to my little house to sleep. We continued to talk about our expectations, our fears, and our hopes for the future. We talked about almost everything.

After tucking Owen into bed one night and giving him all of the time he wanted to share his stories, which he did to put off bedtime, I headed back to the couch and cuddled up against Steve.

"All tucked in?" he asked.

"Like a bug in a rug."

"He's happy."

"I know. So, there's something I've been wanting to talk about," I said.

"Sounds grim."

"It is. Kind of. In the spirit of keeping it real and everything, how are we going to deal with what happened or might have happened while we were separated?"

"You mean if we dated and—"

"Yeah. That. Do you think we should disclose that part if we're to make this work in the long run?"

"I don't see it helping anything," he said. "We were separated. I'd rather not know. You?"

"I don't think I want to know, either. Too much of a slippery slope."

"I'm okay if you're okay," he said.

"I'm okay if you're okay," I said.

"Then, it's settled. Don't ask, don't tell," he joked. "We'll never discuss it."

"It's sealed," I said.

I felt like a teenager again, with butterflies in my stomach, counting the hours until I saw him while I tried to busy myself at work. He texted me throughout my workday. *I miss you. Are you coming over tonight? Thinking of you.* I had a permanent grin on my face and felt like I was floating instead of walking. Dating each other, we had fallen in love all over again. I now spent very little time at the small house between work, writing in cafes, and running at the Y.

We snuggled on the couch with our hands on each other while we watched whatever was on TV.

"So, I was thinking that maybe you should move back in," he said with his head still facing the TV, letting a huge smile cross his face.

"Seriously?"

"A hundred percent," he said, putting his lips on mine.

As I packed up the boxes again, I couldn't believe that I was happily going back to the suburbs. I had been so eager to leave it all behind, I never thought I would ever be raring to live there, and with the man I had left so unquestionably just five months before.

I rummaged through the boxes and found our wedding photos, the ones that had stayed hidden in my basement. I sat on the floor and examined our faces, our genuine happiness. I traced the outline of our bodies with my finger and wiped my tears one last time. I carefully wrapped them back up and sealed the package with tape. I was going back a different person: a whole person with new goals and new dreams, a new understanding of what marriage and love was and clarity about what we both needed to be happy in our relationship. I had gained a sense of respect for who I was and who I was becoming. The last things I packed in the brown boxes were my journals and typed pages—the words that would continue to fill me for years to come. My stories.

Six weeks after our dinner date, I steered the U-Haul with my books and other belongings back to the court. And one month after that, we renewed our wedding vows—just the three of us, in our home. While the sun was setting and the buds were sprouting in our single maple tree, around a candle in our living room, we held hands as we recited the vows we had written ourselves. Our son stood as our only witness.

Owen handed Steve the ring that had been hidden in his pocket, a diamond anniversary band. Steve held my eyes as he slipped it on my finger. Candlelight danced cheerfully across the faces of my husband and son, and me.

16 | The Private

The day we met, I was nineteen and he was almost twenty. We were both home for Easter weekend. He was on leave from the army and I was on break from university, both out with friends we hadn't seen for a long time. The bar was packed, but I noticed him right away. He stood out from the crowd: long legs, beautiful brown skin, and warm, brown eyes. He was smiling—no, laughing—with his friends. They were all much shorter than he was, which made him seem even taller, like a giant. He wore a long-sleeved shirt, but I could tell he was muscular. Strong. I looked at him and he caught me peeking. I smiled and made eye contact, my brown eyes on his, but only for a microsecond. Even so, it was long enough for him to notice I was interested.

"I think I'm going to ask that guy to dance," I said to my friend, biting down on my lip, trying to hide my exhilaration.

"Really? I dare you," she said. She didn't have to. I knew I'd do it. Something inside me told me so. Insisted.

After another drink, I searched for him in the crowded bar. I found him and his friends; they had moved closer to the dance floor. My heart thumped as I strolled towards him. He was wide-eyed, listening to his friend tell a story, probably about a girl he had met the weekend before. He smiled at me as he watched me moving in closer towards him, liquid courage pulsing through my veins. I beamed back.

"Do you want to dance?" I asked, not even introducing myself.

He grinned, making his cheeks puff out like two little apples. "Sure," he said, as he looked at me, then at his friends. I could tell they had a bet to see how long it would take before one of them picked up. "Lead the way," he said.

I grabbed his hand, folded it inside mine, and felt a sudden quiver in my belly, followed by a swift knowing that his hand was meant to be mine. We made our way through the crowd of people holding their drinks and swaying their bodies to the music. We danced to a fast song and then a slow one and then two more. He didn't let me go. He brought me in close, my heart beating against his, my arms draped around his neck and his encircled around my waist. Our bodies were warm against each other, in sync. We shared sound bites of information as the music vibrated. He served in the army, the infantry: a private. I went to school, university: Women's Studies. He thanked me for the dances, lingered a little after the slow songs came to a stop. We exchanged first names. But that was all. It was time for me to go.

"Maybe I'll see you around," he said, his eyes catching the light.

"Maybe," I answered, stepping away from the dance floor. "If it's meant to be."

I thought about him every day, annoyed with myself for not getting his last name or his number. I wanted to know more about this guy who was from the North like me but no longer lived at home. Why hadn't I ever seen him before?

Two weeks later, back at university, my roommate begged me to go out to her favourite bar. I refused at first, and then finally gave in. It was the end of my first year and I was growing tired of the same scene. That was the night she told me to turn around.

"Check him out," she said, her mouth loose and open, awestruck by what stood behind me. I spun around and saw him, overcome by his presence, his confidence. Here he was again before me, five hundred kilometres away from the place where we had first met. Even more handsome then I had remembered. He strutted towards me, grinning from ear to ear, as if he'd been hoping to find me, too.

"Do you want to dance?" he asked, reaching for my hand.

My stomach fluttered. "Lead the way."

"I guess it was meant to be," he whispered.

"Yes," I said.

Acknowledgements

Many thanks to early readers Julie Paul and Anne Boulton. The first drafts are always the scariest. Thank you for saying it didn't suck. A warm thank you to Sarah Selecky, for creating your online course Story is a State of Mind. As a northerner with limited to no writing classes available nearby, this course was a lifeline. Thank you to Steph VanderMeulen, for your editing support and uplifting words as I completed the final draft. This book is better because of you.

Thank you to the Banff Centre for the Arts, where the first story of this memoir was workshopped; the last story was written over long layovers at the airports to and from the centre.

Big happy thank yous to both *Room* magazine and *Event* magazine, where two of my stories were previously published; *Free Fall* and *Operation Release*.

Many thank yous to all those online and in person who have encouraged me along the way with high fives and kind words, especially Shannon Moroney, whom I met at a crucial time while writing this book. Your class Writing What Hurts was key to aiding me during the arduous process of writing these true stories.

To Laura Stradiotto and Heather Campbell, I thank you both so much for standing behind this book and supporting women's stories—thank you for your trust, your courage and for being on my team.

To Gerry Kingsley, for your friendship and stunning photography for the cover. You are a storyteller. To Lauren and Matt Foy, for saying yes.

Friends who also write make this writing thing feel less lonely, and I am immensely grateful to you all: Kim Fahner, Liisa Kovala, Jill Mackenzie, Sofi Papamarko, and Natalie Morill. Thank you especially to Kim, Liisa and Jill, for your close reading and thoughtful suggestions. Thank you as well to those I sat among at the *Fromagerie* during the very early years of this book—my sci-fi writers' group, especially Andy Taylor. You guys were there when it all began. To my Lemontree peeps, thank-you for your loving support.

Profound gratitude and immeasurable appreciation to Merilyn Simonds, my mentor and editor, during this long writing process. I count my lucky stars for crossing paths with you in Banff and being under your caring guidance. You have helped me bring these stories from the depths of darkness. Your encouragement gave me the confidence to move forward—thank you for fiercely championing this book. Your support has been instrumental. You have helped me become a writer.

Deepest thanks to Melanie Hunt, my first reader and dearest friend. Thank you for your keen eye, your listening ear, and for picking up the phone even when you knew it was going to be one of those days when you pushed me through another difficult story. This book would not have been possible without you. Your unwavering faith sustained me. Thank you for loving me despite my many, many flaws.

To Mom, you have always believed in my words and my need to string them into stories. Thanks for being my biggest cheerleader.

To Owen, you are by far the best part of my day. Thank you for your patience while I worked on this book.

To Steve, my love, thank you for giving me the space and time to write about our personal journey. Your tireless support fuelled me as I pushed through each stage of this book. Your encouragement throughout this process has meant everything.

Here's to beating all the odds and to happy endings.
Here's to new beginnings.

Printed by Imprimerie Gauvin
Gatineau, Québec